JOURNAL OF

A RESIDENCE ON A

GEORGIAN PLANTATION

IN 1838–1839

FRANCES ANNE KEMBLE

JOURNAL OF

A RESIDENCE ON A

GEORGIAN PLANTATION

IN 1838–1839

Frances Anne Kemble

with an introduction by
Charles E. Wynes

A BEEHIVE PRESS BOOK

Library of Georgia

SAVANNAH

1992

Published 1992 by The Beehive Foundation

This book was edited by The Beehive Press,
which retains all rights to its design and special contents.
This book is published by The Beehive Foundation
without profit or compensation to The Beehive Press.
The Beehive Foundation gives copies of its books
to college and public libraries throughout Georgia
and also sells them to individuals by mail.

LIBRARY OF GEORGIA
c/o THE BEEHIVE FOUNDATION
321 BARNARD STREET
SAVANNAH, GEORGIA 31401

Frontispiece portrait of Frances Anne Kemble
is reproduced from the collection of
The Brooklyn Museum of Art

CONTENTS

INTRODUCTION

JUST BEFORE CHRISTMAS, 1838, on the 21st of December, a well-dressed family of four accompanied by an English nursemaid boarded a train in Philadelphia, bound for Baltimore on the first leg of a journey that would take them from the winter snow and cool formality of one of America's leading cities, to sunny, informal, almost frontier-like coastal Georgia; from a land of tight-fisted Quaker merchants who had long been in the vanguard of the abolition movement, to a land of cotton and rice planters, and slavery.

Pierce Mease Butler, twenty-eight, whose aristocratic roots rested in South Carolina and Georgia as well as in Philadelphia, was going to Georgia to take possession of two plantations, one primarily a producer of rice and the other of long-staple cotton, that had been left to him and his brother John by their grandfather Major Pierce Butler. Accompanying Butler, over his opposition, were his twenty-nine-year-old wife, the former Frances Anne Kemble, and their two children, Sally, age three, and Frances, just seven months. The elder Frances, known as Fanny, was already famous as a leading Shakespearean actress; the elder daughter, Sally, would be remembered as the mother of the novelist Owen Wister; and Frances, "Fan," the younger, would succeed as a plantation operator in her own right. Pierce Butler would continue to lead a life mired in marital and financial difficulties.

Fanny Kemble was born into one of England's leading theatrical families, on November 27, 1809, the third child of Charles Kemble and Marie Therese Kemble. Following her debut in the role of Juliet, in 1829, she became an overnight sensation. In the fall of 1832, she and her father opened their first American tour to the same adulation she had already received in Europe, including a visit with President Andrew Jackson. Although her American tour might have continued indefinitely, it ended nearly two years later, on June 7, 1834, with her marriage to Pierce Mease Butler, which resulted in temporary abandonment of her theatrical career.

So, in December, 1838, Fanny was on a train in a strange land, bound for an even stranger part of that land, and complaining about the intense cold, the overheated cars, the small seats, the tobacco chewers, the peddlers of various foods at every stop, the over-feeding of American children. At Baltimore, they boarded a steamer, on which Fanny spent a "wretched night," before arriving in Portsmouth, Virginia, the next morning. There, she saw her first slaves, and her reaction, instead of being one of anger and sorrow at their plight, was instead a dispassionate observation upon their dirtiness and the "lazy recklessness" with which they comported themselves.

Then it was on by rail through the wilderness. She found both Virginia and North Carolina to be dirty and unkempt, with poor soil and miserable food; and then, somewhere in North Carolina, the rails ended, to be followed by transportation by horsedrawn coach, until once more there was a railroad. At Wilmington, another steamer was boarded, this time for Charleston. That city fared somewhat better under the lash of Fanny's biting criticism, but she expressed no remorse at leaving it by steamer for Savannah. Arriving in Savannah in a pouring rain, they stayed at the Pulaski House. Then it was by steamer, once more, to Darien, just across the north branch of the Altamaha River from Butler's Island, the family rice plantation, where they soon arrived in a boat that had met them in Darien. It was Sunday, December 30, 1838, and Fanny Kemble was "home" at her husband's plantation.[1]

The little town of Darien had a colorful and varied history. Originally settled by Scotch Highlanders in 1736, Darien became an entrepot for the hinterlands as well as the surrounding coastal area. Lumber, cotton and rice were the chief exports, and the tiny town for a while had hopes of becoming a major seaport and commercial center; but it lost out to both Savannah to the north and Brunswick to the south. Erosion, fire and hurricanes had taken their toll on Darien, and when Fanny Kemble arrived the town was suffering the effects of the Panic of 1837.[2]

Butler's Island, comprising some fifteen hundred acres, was one of many rice and long-staple cotton plantations south of Darien and the northernmost arm of the Altamaha River. By 1760, both the coastal area to the north toward Savannah and the islands to the south had been well settled, but the coastal mainland south of Darien was still a wilderness, claimed by both South Carolina and Georgia till 1763, when, by royal proclamation, the disputed area was awarded to Georgia. The governor of

South Carolina had made numerous land grants there, many of which were allowed to stand so long as the owners met the "clear and cultivate" regulations of Georgia. Thus South Carolina surnames like Middleton, Laurens and others came to mark coastal Georgia as well.

It was through the Middletons that the Butler family came to own Butler's Island, "Woodville," up the river from Butler's Island, and "Hampton," on St. Simons Island, about twenty miles to the south. Major Pierce Butler, the Irish-born grandfather of the husband of Fanny Kemble, had married Mary ("Polly") Middleton in 1771, and following her death in 1790 Major Butler built a mansion at "Hampton," where he spent the winter and spring, with summer and autumn spent at his Philadelphia home, on the corner of Chestnut and Eighth streets. The "Hampton" house was described by a visitor as "an imposing mansion, luxurious, and hospitable," with a guest house nearby known as the "Hill House." Round about there were the usual shops, storehouses, barns and slave quarters. The grounds were formal, with a sunken garden, groves of orange trees and hedges of oleander and boxwood.

No such accommodations ever existed at Butler's Island, where there was only an overseer's cottage, for that plantation, devoted to the production of rice, was a "working plantation" only. The truth is that, compared to rice culture, the cultivation of tobacco and cotton—the other chief cash crops in the pre-Civil War South—was child's play. Rice cultivation involved wet, dirty, unhealthy work; and so heavy was the ditching and banking that, after the war, free Negroes often refused to do it, and Irish laborers from the North had to be imported for the purpose.[3]

Added to the harshness of the cultivation of rice under even the best of circumstances, on Butler's Island there was the additional problem of absentee ownership, with operation of the plantation left in the hands of an overseer. From 1802 until 1838, Roswell King, a native of Northampton, Massachusetts, held the post of Butler's Island overseer, assisted by his son, Roswell King, Jr. In 1838 the Kings resigned and moved to the area north of the future city of Atlanta, where they founded the town of Roswell; but within a few years the younger King returned and continued to operate the plantation into the mid-1850s. In part, it was probably the resignation of the Kings that brought Pierce Butler south to oversee his holdings.

Neither before nor during her visit to Georgia did Fanny Kemble make any secret of her disdain for the institution of slavery. And almost immediately upon arrival at Butler's Island, Fanny became, in the eyes of her husband, a disruptive influence. She persisted in listening to the grievances of the slaves, then carrying those complaints to him, and she was always giving them flannel cloth, soap, "pretties" and other objects that they otherwise never would have known. Finally, Butler ordered her to cease all such discourse and trafficking with the slaves, and declared that she was only making them less content with their lot in life, while not really helping them at all.

Fanny's journal, written in the form of letters to a friend, describes plantation life on Butler's Island and St. Simons. An attitude of moral outrage suffuses all the journal, except when she was describing the natural beauty of Butler's and St. Simons islands and the surrounding marshes, rivers and ocean. On April 17, 1839,

Fanny made the last entry in her journal. It is from this three and one-half months' witness of the "peculiar institution" in a small, isolated section of Georgia—on two large, absentee-owned plantations, where hundreds of Negroes worked in gangs—that there emerged one of the most controversial and widely read descriptions of American Negro slavery.

Was her account a reasonable representation of American Negro slavery? Except for small and occasional minor inaccuracies of fact, there is no reason to doubt the validity of what she described. As to whether it was a fair and accurate description of slavery generally, that is a somewhat different question, though the Civil War generation in the South which first read the journal did not think so. Let us simply say that Fanny Kemble's journal seems to be a reliable description of one face of a many-faceted institution.

Of course, slavery as it existed under the unusually harsh physical conditions of a rice plantation, as on Butler's Island, or on an island plantation devoted to the production of long-staple cotton, as at "Hampton," was a world away from a Virginia or Carolina farm where the owner worked alongside the one or handful of slaves that he owned. It was different even from that of a large inland plantation, whether in Virginia or Georgia, Mississippi or Alabama, where there was close owner-supervision, passed on from generation to generation; and certainly it was even more different from that of the wealthy mercantile families of Savannah or New Orleans who owned only a few of the most intelligent house servants. Fanny Kemble's description of slavery should be viewed with that perspective.

It was not, however, until 1863, in the midst of the

Civil War, that Georgia and the rest of the world got to read the journal. In the meantime, back in Philadelphia and in England, Fanny Kemble's marriage to Pierce Butler was foundering. It is doubtful if she had the temperament for marriage to anyone—unless he had been one content to walk in her shadow—and Pierce Butler was the antithesis of that. With a dominant personality, Butler, in almost feudal fashion, demanded absolute obedience to his will from all those for whom he was responsible, while Fanny, on the other hand, had been in lifelong revolt against authority, and she believed that marriage was a partnership of equals. Such views, when held so strongly by two people, could lead only to conflict; and apparently from the beginning their marital relationship was a stormy one, which the winter in Georgia served only to worsen. An abolitionist and an independent woman accustomed to earning her own way in life, Fanny had now seen at first hand the black backs of slavery upon which her life of relative comfort and ease rested.

So they quarreled, and Butler spent the next winter, 1839–40, alone in Georgia. In December, 1840, the whole family went to England. They remained in England until May, 1843, when they returned, with their relationship unimproved. By then, Fanny was worried about her husband's financial extravagances. In the autumn of 1843 she also discovered evidence that, early in their marriage, Butler had carried on some kind of relationship with another woman. She separated from him, but did not seek a divorce, while they continued to live in the same boarding house but in different apartments. The next spring, on April 15, 1844, Butler fought a duel with James Schott of Philadelphia in Bladensburg, Maryland, where dueling was legal, over Schott's charge that Butler had disrupted the peace and tranquillity of his household—philandering, a less discreet age would have called it. Both men fired but nobody was hit, while honor was saved. A month later, Butler moved out, taking both children with him. In September, 1845, Fanny sailed for England and did not return until May, 1848. Meanwhile, in March, 1848, Butler filed for divorce, and, after long and protracted proceedings, charges and counter charges and threats of a jury trial to determine the facts, the divorce was granted in September, 1849. Fanny was to receive $1500 a year from her former husband and to have custody of the children Sarah and Frances for two months each year.

The divorce made it possible for Fanny to return to the stage, and in the succeeding years she reached the height of her fame, notably as a dramatic reader of Shakespeare. Dividing her time between Europe and America—mostly Europe but especially England—when Fanny was in the United States and between engagements, she often retreated to a cottage she had purchased in Lenox, Massachusetts, the site of a literary colony. It was at Lenox that her daughters sometimes spent part of the summer with her, but this could not have happened often, since she was out of the United States for the entire period from the summer of 1850 to May 1856.[4]

While Fanny was roaming the world, what of her former husband and the Georgia plantations? Possessed of little or no business acumen, Butler had led a life of financial extravagance marked by speculation and gambling as well. Enormous debts were the result. The profits from the Georgia plantations were declining, especially from "Hampton" on St. Simons. Even before Fanny Kemble's visit in 1838–39, "Hampton" was in decline. Long-staple, coastal-grown cotton was giving way to short-staple, upland-grown cotton, and "Hampton" was not suitable for rice cultivation; so the seat of the Georgia operations had shifted to Butler's Island. When Roswell King, Jr., the longtime overseer, left for good in the mid-1850s, even the profitable rice operations on Butler's Island and at "Woodville" became less so. Meanwhile, the number of slaves continued to increase, which constituted an added and growing expense. So, when the financial panic of 1857 hit, it tipped the balance, and Butler was forced—if he was to pay his debts—to sell off 429 slaves of all ages and both sexes. That number represented his half of the total number of slaves; the remainder were retained by the widow of Pierce's brother, John, who had jointly owned the Georgia plantations until his death in 1847.[5]

The auction was held in Savannah, some sixty miles north of Darien, where there were hotel facilities and transportation for buyers who came from all over the South. Mortimer Thomson described the auction for the New York *Tribune*, probably the leading liberal newspaper in the country. The publisher of the *Tribune* was Horace Greeley, brilliant, eccentric and rabidly abolitionist. The auction took place on March 2–3, 1859, and six days later, on March 9th, the nearly 200,000 readers of the *Tribune* were treated to a full description of this example of "Southern decadence" at its worst, although in this instance the slave sale was by a member of one of Philadelphia's finest old families! Later, during the war, shortly after Fanny Kemble's journal was published,

Thomson's account was reprinted under the title, *What Became of the Slaves on a Georgia Plantation: A Sequel to Mrs. Kemble's Journal.*

After the slaves were brought to Savannah, they were quartered in the barns at the race track, some three miles out of town. Their few worldly possessions, including eating and drinking utensils, each family or single person carried in a box or boxes. No light mulattoes were among them, as nearly all were jet-black, while in addition to the field hands there were carpenters, coopers, blacksmiths and shoemakers.

Outside it was pouring rain as the auction got underway. The highest price paid for any one family was $6180 for Sally Walker and her five, mostly grown, children. The highest single price paid was $1750 for William, a "fair carpenter and caulker." "There were," wrote Thomson, "some thirty babies in the lot; they are esteemed worth to the master a hundred dollars the day they are born, and to increase in value at the rate of a hundred dollars a year till they are sixteen or seventeen years old, at which age they bring the best prices." Of a female slave who had given birth just two weeks before she, her husband and three-year-old daughter were put on the block, Thomson bitterly wrote: "It was very considerate in Daphney to be sick [and delivered of a baby] before the sale, for her wailing babe was worth to Mr. Butler all of a hundred dollars." Daphney, her husband, Primus, a carpenter, and their two children brought $2,500. In all, Butler realized $303,850 from the sale. But before the sometimes wailing and weeping slaves were taken away to their new homes all over the South, Butler gave to each of them a dollar, in the form of four brand-new twenty-five-cent pieces. Just as the sale ended, the two days of pouring rain ceased, and the broker, a Mr. Bryan, produced baskets filled with bottles of champagne, and all of the gentlemen were invited to partake.

The sale took place in that strange mixture of cruelty, inhumanity, kindness and even love that marked the institution of slavery in the American South. For instance, years later, Butler's daughter Frances proudly related how some of those very Negroes who had been sold, but who had subsequently found their way back home, explained to a disbelieving Freedman's Bureau agent how they trusted their former master when he said that they could keep all the crops they had already planted before he arrived. "No, sir," said one. "Our master is a just man; he has never lied to us, and we believe him." Surprised, the agent turned to an old former driver named Bram, and asked him how he could have so much faith in a man who had once sold him, to which Bram replied: "Yes, sir, he sold me and I was very unhappy, but he came to me and said, 'Bram, I am in great trouble; I have no money and I have to sell some of the people, but I know where you are all going to, and will buy you back again as soon as I can.' And sir, he told me, Juba, my old wife, must go with me, for though she was not strong, and the gentleman who bought me would not buy her, master said he could not let man and wife be separated; and so, sir, I said, 'Master, if you will keep me I will work for you as long as I live, but if you in trouble and it will help you to sell me, sell me, master, I am willing.' And now that we free, I come back to my old home and my old master, and stay here till I die."[6]

When war came, just two years later, it was not surprising that Butler felt a degree of Southern sympathy, even though, at age fifty-one, he made no move to serve or support either side by taking up arms. In April, 1861, just before Fort Sumter was fired upon, Butler, together with his daughter Frances, visited his Georgia properties. Of the trip, Fanny Kemble declared: "Mr. Butler has gone to swear allegiance to the Southern Confederacy and to establish himself on his plantation again." Back in Philadelphia in August, however, Butler was arrested and charged with treason. The federal government claimed that, while in the South, Butler had received large amounts of money with which he was to purchase Confederate munitions; and he was imprisoned at Fort LaFayette in New York. Five weeks later, after taking an oath of allegiance to the United States and pledging that he would not go South again during the war without a passport from the Secretary of State, he was released. Apparently feeling himself to have been grievously wronged, the next year Butler unsuccessfully sought to sue the Secretary of War, Simon Cameron, for trespass, assault and battery, and false arrest. For the remainder of the war nothing further was heard about Butler's loyalty, but he did do much work to alleviate the lot of Confederate prisoners held in the North.[7]

The Civil War, of course, found Fanny Kemble in support of the North, but a visit to England in 1862 left her both appalled and chagrined at the widespread support for the Confederacy—in her England, which had for so long been an antislavery bastion. It was for this reason that, primarily for the English public, she decided to publish her journal. In May, 1863, the English edition appeared, and in July the North also gained whatever moral suasion that might be attached to the appearance of so damning an account of slavery as was contained in the journal with its publication in America.

Just what was the impact of publication of the journal upon English foreign policy, since so many of the English upper class made no secret of their sympathy for the Confederacy and its aristocracy? The question cannot really be answered, though many Southerners bitterly believed that through publication of her journal, "Fanny Kemble single-handedly prevented England's recognition of the Confederacy," a belief that her adoring and uncritical biographers have perpetuated. The truth is, that by mid-1863, all serious hope for intervention by the English was already past. The Emancipation Proclamation of January 1, five months before the journal was first published in England, finally made the Civil War a moral issue, in addition to the more practical issue of simply keeping the Union together, and it brought the rising English working class, with its antislavery background, loudly to the side of the North. In early July, two months after English publication and just as the American edition was about to appear, the Confederacy was cut in two at the Battle of Vicksburg, and Confederate invasion of the North was turned back at Gettysburg. The journal probably was widely circulated among those English workers who could read and among others who sympathized with the North—as much perhaps as an indictment of aristocracy in general, as an antislavery tract—but it was not needed to turn the tide of English sentiment; and if it had ever been needed, it came too late.

The effect upon American opinion of publication of the journal is even less certain, but a second printing was made in 1864.[8] In the flush of victories at Vicksburg and Gettysburg, as well as Northern wartime prosperity, the Northern reading public might well have been expected to readily devour such a well-told tale about the iniquities of the enemy who was now clearly doomed to defeat. At any rate, Fanny Kemble's place in history was now doubly secure—as a Shakespearean actress and reader, and as propagandist for the cause of abolition. Americans ever since, including Southerners, have had a sort of love-hate relationship for this haughty English actress, who never sought to conceal her disdain for so much about America and Americans, but above all for the institution of slavery.

As for the Georgia plantations, the war years saw them neglected and left to all but grow up wild. Just a year after the cessation of hostilities, Butler decided to go South once more to claim the remains of his estate. Leaving Philadelphia on March 22nd, 1866, he was accompanied by his younger daughter, Frances, or "Fan," who, like her father, had been a Southern sympathizer during the war, and who, also like him, had her differences with her mother, Fanny Kemble. The trip overland to Savannah was completed by rail, but also by carriage and wagon where the railroads had been torn up. From Savannah, they went by boat to Darien and arrived at Butler's Island twenty-seven years and three months after Fanny Kemble first set foot upon that plantation.

That year and the next, Butler and his daughter struggled to make a rice crop with free Negro labor, with both sides thoroughly confused and frustrated by the "new order of things." But before the second crop was harvested, in August, 1867, Butler died, apparently of malaria. He was buried in Darien amidst the lamentations of some of his former slaves. Later, his body was removed to Philadelphia.

Until the end of the year 1876 Frances continued successfully to run the rice plantation on Butler's Island; the long-staple cotton plantation on St. Simons Island she gave up after 1869 and rented the land for nominal amounts to the former slaves there. After 1871, when Frances married the Reverend James Wentworth Leigh, an English clergyman, she turned over operation of the plantation to her husband. In January, 1877, the Leighs left Butler's Island and returned to England.

Then, like her mother, Fanny Kemble, Frances wrote an account of her experience as plantation mistress, which was published in London in 1883 under the title, *Ten Years on a Georgia Plantation Since the War*. Frances claimed that she never read her mother's *Journal*, because it might have caused her to come to "hate" its author. Whether Fanny ever read her daughter's account is unknown.

Meanwhile, though Fanny several times returned to the United States, mostly to visit friends and her elder daughter, Sally, who had married Dr. Owen J. Wister of Philadelphia, she never returned to Georgia. Frances, while still in Georgia, had to see her mother in Philadelphia or elsewhere. The relationship between the two was strained anyway, since "Fan" was truly a doting father's daughter, later naming her first short-lived son after him.

The last twenty years of Fanny's life saw her develop one of the richest and most rewarding friendships of her entire life—with Henry James, to whom she was introduced in Rome, in 1873, by her elder daughter, Sarah. Fanny was older than James by thirty-four years, but this age difference did not keep them from a relationship as intellectual equals, as well as one of genuine friendship.

In 1879 James wrote to his mother concerning Fanny: "Mrs. Kemble has returned to town [London] for the winter—an event in which I always take pleasure, as she is certainly one of the women I know whom I like best. . . . a woman who (extremely annoying as she sometimes is) gives one a positive sense of having a deep, rich human nature and having cast off all vulgarities. The people of this world seem to me for the most part nothing but surface, and sometimes—oh, ye gods! such desperately poor surface. Mrs. Kemble has no organized surface at all; she is like a straight, deep cistern without a cover, or even, sometimes, a bucket into which, as a mode of intercourse, one must tumble with a splash."[9] Then, following Fanny's death at age eighty-three, in London, on January 15th, 1893, James wrote that "her talk reflected a thousand vanished and present things. It swarmed with people and with criticism of people, with the ghosts of a dead society. She had, in two hemispheres, seen everyone and known everyone, had assisted at the social comedy of her age."[10]

On Butler's Island the tides still ceaselessly rise and fall and batter at the remains of the old dikes, just as they did when Fanny Kemble watched them some one hundred-fifty years ago, while the banks of the canals still burst with a profusion of color in the spring. Only that natural world of beauty that she so lyrically described has survived.

CHARLES E. WYNES

Frances Anne Kemble's *Journal of a Residence on a Georgian Plantation* was published at London and New York in 1863. This Beehive Press volume is based on the 1863 New York edition. Concentrating on Fanny Kemble's firsthand observations of plantation life, our new edition deletes paragraphs on other subjects (for example, a long secondhand account of the wreck of the steamship *Pulaski*), comments on people, places and things in England and some of her most hyperbolic or condescending comments about slavery or slaves in general. To enhance continuity, the greetings and farewells in Mrs. Kemble's "letters" that form her journal have been deleted. The author's generally critical tone has not been changed, and all specific critical observations of slavery and slaves have been retained. The names of many persons, identified in the original text only by mysterious initials, have been filled in. To the original text, a few opening paragraphs that describe the arrival at Butler's Island have been added from Kemble's *Records of Later Life* (London, 1882). Readers who wish to read the complete text are reminded that it was reprinted with an introduction by John A. Scott in 1961.

1. Frances Anne Kemble, *Journal of a Residence on a Georgian Plantation in 1838–1839*, ed. with an Introduction by John A. Scott (New York: Alfred A. Knopf, Inc., 1961), pp. 12–50.

2. Burnette Vanstory, *Georgia's Land of the Golden Isles* (Athens: University of Georgia Press, 1956), pp. 59–71.

3. One useful and accurate, if highly romantic, description of rice culture along the Altamaha is this one: "The fertile delta lands were ideally suited for growing rice: far enough from the sea for the water to have lost the strong salt that would have damaged the grain, yet near enough for the ebb and flow of the tide to be an advantage in flooding the low lying fields. . . . Vast acres of marshland were drained, ditches and canals dug, dikes and levees built, sluice-gates and locks constructed. Strong embankments had to be thrown up completely around the river islands, as they often lay two or three feet below the crest of the water at high tide. . . .

"Rice was planted in March, April, and May, and the fields were flooded at full moon and new moon when the tides always run high. A big event of the plantation was "claying" the seed rice. The grain was spread upon the floor of the rice barn and covered with a thick mixture of clay and water. Then the slaves, young and old, had a 'shout'—a sort of dance where they shuffled barefoot over the rice, clapping, singing, and chanting. Visitors to the plantations wrote of having seen similar performances when traveling in Egypt. When the shout was over the grains of seed rice were covered with the heavy clay which would keep them from floating until they took root.

"As soon as the grain was sowed the sluice-gates were opened and the tide was allowed to cover the fields. Then the gates were closed and the rice was left to sprout. The fields were drained when the green shoots showed above the shallow water—a pretty sight, the acres of new green, the

xxiv

banks blooming with wild violets and with a tangle of yellow jasmine and wild blackberry. Constant work was required to keep the fields clear of 'careless grass' and weeds, to give the rice its exact amount of water [two more "flows" or flooding], to keep canals and ditches dug out, and locks and sluice-gates in repair against the continual force of the tide. . . .

"As the grain ripened there was the added task of trying to protect it from the flocks of little rice birds that descended at dawn upon the fields. Boys [i.e. slave boys] stationed on the banks with improvised noisemakers were often joined by the young men of the [planter's] family for the early morning sport of shooting, as the birds were considered a delectable breakfast dish, delicious morsels crisply browned and served with buttered grits and hot biscuits. When the rice was fully matured it was cut and loaded upon flats, long raft-like boats that could be poled along the canals or drawn by oxen from the tow-paths upon the banks. After the harvest had been gathered in [and threshed at the rice mill], the whole plantation celebrated with a feast and 'jubilee,' followed by a well-earned rest." *Ibid.*, 76–7.

4. Leota S. Driver, *Fanny Kemble* (Chapel Hill: University of North Carolina Press, 1933), pp. 115–163.

5. Margaret Armstrong, *Fanny Kemble: A Passionate Victorian* (New York: The Macmillan Company, 1938), pp. 329–30.

6. Frances Butler Leigh, *Ten Years on a Georgia Plantation Since the War* (Savannah: The Beehive Foundation, 1992).

7. Driver, *Fanny Kemble*, p. 177; Armstrong, *Fanny Kemble*, pp. 336–7.

8. Ibid., pp. li–liii.

9. Quoted, *Fanny, the American Kemble: Her Journals and Unpublished Letters*, ed. with annotations by Fanny Kemble Wister (Tallahassee: South Pass Press, 1972), pp. 214–5.

10. Quoted, ibid., p. 215.

The following diary was kept in the winter and spring of 1838–9, on an estate consisting of rice and cotton plantations, in the islands at the entrance of the Altamaha, on the coast of Georgia.

ARRIVAL

DECEMBER 1838 – JANUARY 1839

OUR STEAM-BOAT, *The Ocmulgee*, was a tiny, tidy little vessel. On Sunday morning the day broke most brilliantly over the Southern waters, and as the sun rose, the atmosphere became clear and warm. On either side lay the low reedy swamps, yellow, withered forests, rattling their brittle canes in the morning breeze. Through these dreary banks we wound a most sinuous course for a long time; at length the irregular buildings of the little town of Darien appeared, and as we grazed the side of the wharf it seemed to me as if we had touched the outer bounds of civilized creation. Beyond the broad river and the low swamp lands the savage-looking woods arose to meet the horizon. We seemed to have travelled to the very end of the world.

As soon as we showed ourselves on the deck we were hailed by a shout from the men in two pretty boats, which had pulled alongside of us; and the vociferations of "Oh, massa! how you do, massa? Oh, missis! oh! lily missis! me too glad to see you!" accompanied with shrieks, whoops, whistles and grunts. We were presently transferred into the larger boat, and the smaller one being freighted with our luggage, we pulled off from Darien.

We crossed another arm of the Altamaha and approached the low, reedy banks of Butler's Island, and passed the rice-mill and buildings surrounding it, all of which, it being Sunday, were closed. As we neared the bank, the steersman took up a huge conch and sounded out our approach. The wharf began to be crowded with negroes, jumping, dancing, shouting, laughing, and clapping their hands. On our landing from the boat, the crowd thronged about us like a swarm of bees; we were seized, pulled, pushed, carried, dragged, and all but lifted in the air by the clamorous multitude. They seized our clothes, kissed them—then our hands, and almost wrung them off. I believe I was almost frightened.

If you will take a map of North America and a powerful magnifying glass, you may perceive the small speck known by the title of Butler's Island. The place, which is only a portion of our Georgia estate, contains several thousand acres, and is about eight miles round. The place is one of the wildest corners of creation. The whole island is swamp, a sort of hasty-pudding of amphibious elements, composed of a huge rolling river, thick and turbid with mud, and stretches of mud banks, scarcely reclaimed from the water; diked and trenched and divided by ditches and a canal, by means of which the rice-fields are periodically overflowed, and the harvest transported to the threshing mill.

In taking my first walk on the island, I directed my steps toward the rice mill, a large building on the banks of the river, within a few yards of the house we occupy. The rice mill is worked by a steam-engine of thirty horse power, and, besides threshing great part of our own rice, is kept constantly employed by the neighboring planters, who send their grain to it in preference to the more distant mill at Savannah, paying, of course, the same percentage, which makes it a very profitable addition to the estate. Immediately opposite to this building is a small shed, which they call the cook's shop, and where the daily allowance of rice and corn grits of the people is boiled and distributed to them by an old woman, whose special business this is. There are four settlements or villages (or, as the negroes call them, camps) on the island, consisting of from ten to twenty houses, and to each settlement is annexed a cook's shop with capacious caldrons, and the oldest wife of the settlement for officiating priestess. Pursuing my walk along the river's bank, upon an artificial dike, sufficiently high and broad to protect the fields from inundation by the ordinary rising of the tide—for the whole island is below high-water mark—I passed the blacksmith's and cooper's shops. At the first all the common iron implements of husbandry or household use for the estate are made, and at the latter all the rice barrels necessary for the crop, besides tubs and buckets, large and small, for the use of the people, and cedar tubs, of noble dimensions and exceedingly neat workmanship, for our own household purposes. After this I got out of the vicinity of the settlement, and pursued my way along a narrow dike—the river on the one hand, and, on the other, a slimy, poisonous-looking swamp, all rattling with sedges of enormous height, in which one might lose one's way as effectually as in a forest of oaks. Beyond this, the low rice-fields, all clothed in their rugged stubble, divided by dikes into monotonous squares. My walks are rather circumscribed, inasmuch as the dikes are the only promenades. On all sides of these lie either the marshy rice-fields, the brimming river, or the swampy

3

patches of yet unreclaimed forest, where the huge cypress-trees and exquisite evergreen undergrowth spring up from a stagnant sweltering pool, that effectually forbids the foot of the explorer.

As I skirted one of these thickets to-day, I stood still to admire the beauty of the shrubbery. Every shade of green, every variety of form, every degree of varnish, and all in full leaf and beauty in the very depth of winter. The stunted dark-colored oak; the magnolia bay, which grows to a very great size; the wild myrtle, a beautiful and profuse shrub, rising to a height of six, eight, and ten feet, and branching on all sides in luxuriant tufted fullness; most beautiful of all, that pride of the South, the *magnolia grandiflora*, whose lustrous dark green perfect foliage would alone render it an object of admiration, without the queenly blossom whose color, size, and perfume are unrivaled in the whole vegetable kingdom.

I must inform you of a curious conversation which took place between my little girl and the woman who performs for us the offices of chambermaid here—of course one of Mr. Butler's slaves. What suggested it to the child, or whence indeed she gathered her information, I know not; but children are made of eyes and ears, and nothing, however minute, escapes their microscopic observation. She suddenly began addressing this woman. "Mary, some persons are free and some are not (the woman made no reply). I am a free person (of a little more than three years old). I say, I am a free person, Mary—do you know that?" "Yes, missis." "Some persons are free and some are not—do you know that, Mary?" "Yes, missis, *here,*" was the reply; "I know it is so here, in this world." Here my child's white nurse, my

4

dear Margery, who had hitherto been silent, interfered, saying, "Oh, then you think it will not always be so?" "Me hope not, missis." Oh, if you could imagine how this title "Missis," addressed to me and to my children, shocks all my feelings! Several times I have exclaimed, "For God's sake do not call me that!" and only been awakened, by the stupid amazement of the poor creatures I was addressing, to the perfect uselessness of my thus expostulating with them; once or twice, indeed, I have done more—I have explained to them, and they appeared to comprehend me well, that I had no ownership over them, for that I held such ownership sinful, and that, though I was the wife of the man who pretends to own them, I was, in truth, no more their mistress than they were mine. Some of them I know understood me, more of them did not.

Our servants—those who have been selected to wait upon us in the house—consist of a man, who is quite a tolerable cook; a dairy-woman, who churns for us; a laundry-woman; her daughter, our housemaid, the afore-said Mary; and two young lads of from fifteen to twenty, who wait upon us in the capacity of footmen. As, however, the latter are perfectly filthy in their persons and clothes—their faces, hands, and naked feet being literally incrusted with dirt—their attendance at our meals is not, as you may suppose, particularly agreeable to me, and I dispense with it as often as possible. Mary, too, is so intolerably offensive in her person that it is impossible to endure her proximity, and the consequence is that, among Mr. Butler's slaves, I wait upon myself more than I have ever done in my life before. About this same personal offensiveness, the Southerners, you know, insist that it is inherent with the race, and it is one of their most cogent reasons for keeping them as slaves. This very disagreeable peculiarity does not prevent Southern women from hanging their infants at the breasts of negresses, nor almost every planter's wife and daughter from having one or more little pet blacks sleeping like puppy-dogs in their very bedchamber, nor almost every planter from admitting one or several of his female slaves to the still closer intimacy of his bed. I am strongly inclined to believe that peculiar ignorance of the laws of health and the habits of decent cleanliness are the real and only causes of this disagreeable characteristic of the race. A total absence of self-respect begets these hateful physical results, and in proportion as moral influences are remote, physical evils will abound.

The eldest son of our laundry-woman, and Mary's brother, a boy of the name of Aleck, is uncommonly bright and intelligent; he performs all the offices of a well-instructed waiter with great efficiency, and any where out of slave land would be able to earn fourteen or fifteen dollars a month for himself; he is remarkably good tempered and well disposed. The other poor boy is so stupid that he appears sullen from absolute darkness of intellect. I should tell you that Aleck's parents and kindred have always been about the house of the overseer, and in daily habits of intercourse with him and his wife; and wherever this is the case the effect of involuntary education is evident in the improved intelligence of the degraded race. In a conversation which Mr. Butler had this evening with Mr. O——, the overseer, the latter mentioned that two of our carpenters had in their leisure time made a boat, which they had disposed of to some neighboring planter for sixty dollars.

And here it may be well to inform you that the slaves

on this plantation are divided into field-hands and me-
chanics or artisans. The former, the great majority, are
the more stupid and brutish of the tribe; the others, who
are regularly taught their trades, are not only exceedingly
expert at them, but exhibit a greater general activity of
intellect, which must necessarily result from even a partial degree of cultivation. In the part of Georgia where
this estate is situated, the custom of task labor is universal. These tasks profess to be graduated according to
the sex, age, and strength of the laborer. There are here a
gang (for that is the honorable term) of coopers, of
blacksmiths, of bricklayers, of carpenters, all well acquainted with their peculiar trades. The latter constructed
the wash-hand stands, clothes-presses, sofas, tables, etc.,
with which our house is furnished, and they are very
neat pieces of workmanship—neither veneered or pol-
ished indeed, nor of very costly materials, but of the
white pine wood planed as smooth as marble—a species
of furniture not very luxurious perhaps, but all the better
adapted therefore to the house itself, which is certainly
rather more devoid of the conveniences and adornments
of modern existence than any thing I ever took up my
abode in before.

It consists of three small rooms, and three still smaller,
which would be more appropriately designated as closets,
a wooden recess by way of pantry, and a kitchen de-
tached from the dwelling—a mere wooden out-house,
with no floor but the bare earth, and for furniture a congregation of filthy negroes, who lounge in and out of it
like hungry hounds at all hours of the day and night,
picking up such scraps of food as they can find about.
Of our three apartments, one is our sitting, eating, and
living room, and is sixteen feet by fifteen. The walls are

plastered indeed, but neither painted nor papered; it is divided from our bedroom by a dingy wooden partition covered all over with hooks, pegs, and nails, to which hats, caps, keys, etc., etc., are suspended in graceful irregularity. The doors open by wooden latches, raised by means of small bits of pack-thread. The third room, a chamber with sloping ceiling, immediately over our sitting-room and under the roof, is appropriated to the nurse and my two babies. Of the closets, one is Mr. O——, the overseer's, bedroom, the other his office or place of business; and the third, adjoining our bedroom, and opening immediately out of doors, is Mr. Butler's dressing-room and *cabinet d'affaires*, where he gives audiences to the negroes, redresses grievances, distributes red woolen caps (a singular gratification to a slave), shaves himself, and performs the other offices of his toilet. Such being our abode, I think you will allow there is little danger of my being dazzled by the luxurious splendors of a Southern slave residence. Our sole mode of summoning our attendants is by a pack-thread bell-rope suspended in the sitting-room. From the bedrooms we have to raise the windows and our voices, and bring them by power of lungs, or help ourselves.

I had a most ludicrous visit this morning from the midwife of the estate—rather an important personage both to master and slave, as to her unassisted skill and science the ushering of all the young negroes into their existence of bondage is intrusted. I heard a great deal of conversation in the dressing-room adjoining mine while performing my own toilet, and presently Mr. Butler opened my room door, ushering in a dirty, fat, good-humored looking old negress, saying, "The midwife, Rose, wants to make your acaquintance." "Oh massa!" shrieked out the old creature, in a paroxysm of admiration, "where you get this lilly alabaster baby!" For a moment I looked round to see if she was speaking of my baby; but no, my dear, this superlative apostrophe was elicited by the fairness of *my* skin! Soon after this visit, I was summoned into the wooden porch or piazza of the house, to see a poor woman who desired to speak to me. This was none other than the tall, emaciated-looking negress who, on the day of our arrival, had embraced me and my nurse with such irresistible zeal. She appeared very ill to-day, and presently unfolded to me a most distressing history of bodily afflictions. She was the mother of a very large family, and complained to me that what with childbearing and hard field labor, her back was almost broken in two. With an almost savage vehemence of gesticulation, she suddenly tore up her scanty clothing, and exhibited a spectacle with which I was inconceivably shocked and sickened. I promised to attend to her ailments and give her proper remedies.

After the departure of this poor woman, I walked down the settlement toward the Infirmary or hospital, calling in at one or two of the houses along the row. These cabins consist of one room, about twelve feet by fifteen, with a couple of closets smaller and closer than the state-rooms of a ship, divided off from the main room and each other by rough wooden partitions, in which the inhabitants sleep. They have almost all of them a rude bedstead, with the gray moss of the forests for mattress, and filthy, pestilential-looking blankets for covering. Two families (sometimes eight and ten in number) reside in one of these huts, which are mere wooden frames pinned, as it were, to the earth by a brick chimney outside, whose enormous aperture within pours down a flood of

9

air, but little counteracted by the miserable spark of fire, which hardly sends an attenuated thread of lingering smoke up its huge throat. A wide ditch runs immediately at the back of these dwellings, which is filled and emptied daily by the tide. Attached to each hovel is a small scrap of ground for a garden, which, however, is for the most part untended and uncultivated. Such of these dwellings as I visited to-day were filthy and wretched in the extreme, and exhibited that most deplorable consequence of ignorance and an abject condition, the inability of the inhabitants to secure and improve even such pitiful comfort as might yet be achieved by them.

Instead of the order, neatness, and ingenuity which might convert even these miserable hovels into tolerable residences, there was careless, reckless, filthy indolence. Firewood and shavings lay littered about the floors, while the half-naked children were cowering round two or three smouldering cinders. The moss with which the chinks and crannies of their ill-protecting dwellings might have been stuffed was trailing in dirt and dust about the ground, while the back door of the huts, opening upon a most unsightly ditch, was left wide open for the fowls and ducks, which they are allowed to raise, to travel in and out, increasing the filth of the cabin by what they brought and left in every direction. In the midst of the floor, or squatting round the cold hearth, would be four or five little children from four to ten years old, the latter all with babies in their arms, the care of the infants being taken from the mothers (who are driven afield as soon as they recover from child labor), and devolved upon these poor little nurses, as they are called, whose business it is to watch the infant, and carry it to its mother whenever it may require nourishment. To these hardly human little beings I addressed my remonstrances about the filth, cold, and unnecessary wretchedness of their room, bidding the elder boys and girls kindle up the fire, sweep the floor, and expel the poultry. For a long time my very words seemed unintelligible to them, till, when I began to sweep and make up the fire, etc., they first fell to laughing, and then imitating me. The incrustations of dirt on their hands, feet, and faces were my next object of attack, and the stupid negro practice of keeping the babies with their feet bare, and their heads, already well capped by nature with their woolly hair, wrapped in half a dozen hot, filthy coverings. Thus I traveled down the "street." My heart is full almost to bursting as I walk among these most poor creatures.

The Infirmary is a large two-story building, terminating the broad orange-planted space between the two rows of houses which form the first settlement; it is built of whitewashed wood, and contains four large-sized rooms. But how shall I describe to you the spectacle which was presented to me on entering the first of these? But half the casements, of which there were six, were glazed, and these were obscured with dirt, almost as much as the other windowless ones were darkened by the dingy shutters, which the shivering inmates had fastened to in order to protect themselves from the cold. In the enormous chimney glimmered the powerless embers of a few sticks of wood, round which, however, as many of the sick women as could approach were cowering, some on wooden settles, most of them on the ground, excluding those who were too ill to rise; and these last poor wretches lay prostrate on the floor, without bed, mattress, or pillow, buried in tattered and filthy blankets, which, huddled round them as they lay strewed about, left hardly space to move upon the floor. I stood in the midst of them, perfectly unable to speak, the tears pouring from my eyes at this sad spectacle of their misery, myself and my emotion alike strange and incomprehensible to them. Here lay women expecting every hour the terrors and agonies of childbirth, others who had just brought their doomed offspring into the world, others who were groaning over the anguish and bitter disappointment of miscarriages—here lay some burning with fever, others chilled with cold and aching with rheumatism, upon the hard cold ground, the draughts and dampness of the atmosphere increasing their sufferings, and dirt, noise, and stench, and every aggravation of which sickness is capable, combined in their condition—here they lay like brute beasts.

As soon as I recovered from my dismay, I addressed old Rose the midwife, who had charge of this room, bidding her open the shutters of such windows as were glazed, and let in the light. I next proceeded to make up the fire; but, upon my lifting a log for that purpose, there was one universal outcry of horror, and old Rose, attempting to snatch it from me, exclaimed, "Let alone, missis—let be; what for you lift wood? You have nigger enough, missis, to do it!" I hereupon had to explain to them my view of the purposes for which hands and arms were appended to our bodies, and forthwith began making Rose tidy up the miserable apartment, removing all the filth and rubbish from the floor that could be removed, folding up in piles the blankets of the patients who were not using them, and placing, in rather more sheltered and comfortable positions, those who were unable to rise. It was all that I could do, and having enforced upon them all my earnest desire that they should keep their room swept, and as tidy as possible, I passed on to the other room on the ground floor, and to the two above, one of which is appropriated to the use of the men who are ill. They were all in the same deplorable condition, the upper rooms being rather the more miserable, inasmuch as none of the windows were glazed at all, and they had, therefore, only the alternative of utter darkness, or killing draughts of air from the unsheltered casements. In all, filth, disorder, and misery abounded; the floor was the only bed, and scanty begrimed rags of blankets the only covering.

I left this refuge for Mr. Butler's sick dependents with my clothes covered with dust, and full of vermin, and with a heart heavy enough, as you will well believe. My morning's work had fatigued me not a little, and I was glad to return to the house, where I gave vent to my indignation and regret at the scene I had just witnessed to Mr. Butler and his overseer, who, here, is a member of our family. The latter told me that the condition of the hospital had appeared to him, from his first entering upon his situation (only within the last year), to require a reform, and that he had proposed it to the former manager, Mr. King, and Mr. King's brother, who is part proprietor of the estate, but, receiving no encouragement from them, had supposed that it was a matter of indifference to the owners, and had left it in the condition in which he had found it, in which condition it has been for the last nineteen years and upward. This new overseer of ours has lived fourteen years with an old Scotch gentleman, who owns an estate adjoining Mr. Butler's, on the island of St. Simon's, upon which estate, from every thing I can gather, and from what I know of

13

the proprietor's character, the slaves are probably treated with as much humanity as is consistent with slavery at all, and where the management and comfort of the hospital in particular had been most carefully and judiciously attended to.

I forgot to tell you that in the hospital were several sick babies, whose mothers were permitted to suspend their field labor in order to nurse them. Upon addressing some remonstrances to one of these, who, besides having a sick child, was ill herself, about the horribly dirty condition of her baby, she assured me that it was impossible for them to keep their children clean; that they went out to work at daybreak, and did not get their tasks done till evening, and that then they were too tired and worn out to do any thing but throw themselves down and sleep. This statement of hers I mentioned on my return from the hospital, and the overseer appeared extremely annoyed by it, and assured me repeatedly that it was not true.

In the evening Mr. Butler, who had been over to Darien, mentioned that one of the storekeepers there had told him that, in the course of a few years, he had paid the negroes of this estate several thousand dollars for moss, which is a very profitable article of traffic with them: they collect it from the trees, dry and pick it, and then sell it to the people in Darien for mattresses, sofas, and all sorts of stuffing purposes, which, in my opinion, it answers better than any other material whatever that I am acquainted with, being as light as horse-hair, as springy and elastic, and a great deal less harsh and rigid. It is now bedtime. There is a preliminary to my repose, however, which I rather dread, namely, the hunting for, or discovering without hunting, upon the whitewashed walls of my bedroom, a most hideous and detestable species called centipedes, which come out of the cracks and crevices of the walls, and fill my very heart with dismay. They are from an inch to two inches long, and appear to have not a hundred, but a thousand legs. I can not ascertain very certainly from the negroes whether they sting or not, but they look exceedingly as if they might, and I visit my babies every night in fear and trembling, lest I should find one or more of these hateful creatures mounting guard over them. You are well to be free from centipedes—better to be free from slaves.

MORE EXPLORATIONS

JANUARY 1839

THIS MORNING I paid my second visit to the Infirmary, and found there had been some faint attempt at sweeping and cleaning, in compliance with my entreaties. The poor woman Harriet, however, whose statement with regard to the impossibility of their attending properly to their children had been so vehemently denied by the overseer, was crying bitterly. I asked her what ailed her, when, more by signs and dumb show than words, she and old Rose informed me that Mr. O——had flogged her that morning for having told me that the women had not time to keep their children clean. It is part of the regular duty of every overseer to visit the Infirmary at least once a day, which he generally does in the morning, and Mr. O——'s visit had preceded mine but a short time only, or I might have been edified by seeing a man horsewhip a woman. I again and again made her repeat her story, and she again and again affirmed that she had been flogged for what she told me, none of the whole company in the room denying it or contradicting her. I left the room because I was so disgusted and indignant that I could hardly restrain my feelings, and to express them could have produced no single good result.

In the next ward, stretched upon the ground, apparently either asleep or so overcome with sickness as to be incapable of moving, lay an immense woman; her stature, as she cumbered the earth, must have been, I should think, five feet seven or eight, and her bulk enormous. She was wrapped in filthy rags, and lay with her face on the floor. As I approached, and stooped to see what ailed her, she suddenly threw out her arms, and, seized with violent convulsions, rolled over and over upon the floor, beating her head violently upon the ground, and throwing her enormous limbs about in a horrible manner. Immediately upon the occurrence of this fit, four or five women threw themselves literally upon her, and held her down by main force; they even proceeded to bind her legs and arms together, to prevent her dashing herself about; but this violent coercion and tight bandaging seemed to me, in my profound ignorance, more likely to increase her illness by impeding her breathing and the circulation of her blood, and I bade them desist, and unfasten all the strings and ligatures not only that they had put round her limbs, but which, by tightening her clothes round her body, caused any obstruction. The fit presently subsided, and was succeeded by the most deplorable prostration and weakness of nerves, the tears streaming down the poor woman's cheeks in showers, without, however, her uttering a single word, though she moaned incessantly. After bathing her forehead, hands, and chest with vinegar, we raised her up, and I sent to the house for a chair with a back (there was no such thing in the hospital), and we contrived to place her in it. I have seldom seen finer women than this poor creature and her younger sister, an immense strapping lass called Chloe—tall, straight, and extremely well made

17

—who was assisting her sister, and whom I had remarked, for the extreme delight and merriment which my cleansing propensities seemed to give her, on my last visit to the hospital. She was here taking care of a sick baby, and helping to nurse her sister Molly, who, it seems, is subject to those fits, about which I spoke to our physician here—an intelligent man residing in Darien, who visits the estate whenever medical assistance is required. He seemed to attribute them to nervous disorder, brought on by frequent childbearing. This woman is young, I suppose at the outside not thirty, and her sister informed me that she had had ten children—ten children!

Among the patients in this room was a young girl, apparently from fourteen to fifteen, whose hands and feet were literally rotting away piecemeal, from the effect of a horrible disease, to which the negroes are subject here, and I believe in the West Indies, and when it attacks the joints of the toes and fingers, the pieces absolutely decay and come off, leaving the limb a maimed and horrible stump! Another disease, of which they complained much, and which, of course, I was utterly incapable of accounting for, was a species of lock-jaw, to which their babies very frequently fall victims in the first or second week after their birth, refusing the breast, and the mouth gradually losing the power of opening itself. Pleurisy, or a tendency to it, seems very common among them; also peripneumonia, or inflammation of the lungs, which is terribly prevalent, and generally fatal. Rheumatism is almost universal; and as it proceeds from exposure, and want of knowledge and care, attacks indiscriminately the young and old. A great number of the women are victims to falling of the womb and weakness in the spine; but these are necessary results of their laborious existence, and do not belong either to climate or constitution.

I have proclaimed to all the little baby nurses that I will give a cent to every little boy or girl whose baby's face shall be clean, and one to every individual with clean face and hands of their own. My appeal was fully comprehended by the majority, it seems, for this morning I was surrounded, as soon as I came out, by a swarm of children carrying their little charges on their backs and in their arms, the shining, and, in many instances, wet faces and hands of the latter bearing ample testimony to the ablutions which had been inflicted upon them.

At the upper end of the row of houses, and nearest to our overseer's residence, is the hut of the head driver. Let me explain, by the way, his office. The negroes, as I before told you, are divided into troops or gangs, as they are called; at the head of each gang is a driver, who stands over them, whip in hand, while they perform their daily task, who renders an account of each individual slave and his work every evening to the overseer, and receives from him directions for their next day's tasks. Each driver is allowed to inflict a dozen lashes upon any refractory slave in the field, and at the time of the offense; they may not, however, extend the chastisement, and if it is found ineffectual, their remedy lies in reporting the unmanageable individual either to the head driver or the overseer, the former of whom has power to inflict three dozen lashes at his own discretion, and the latter as many as he himself sees fit, within the number of fifty; which limit, however, I must tell you, is an arbitrary one on this plantation, appointed by the founder of the estate, Major Butler, Mr. Butler's grandfather, many of whose regulations, indeed I believe most of them, are still observed in the government of the plantation. Limits of this sort, however, to the power of either driver, head driver, or overseer, may or may not exist elsewhere; they are, to a certain degree, a check upon the power of these individuals; but in the absence of the master, the overseer may confine himself within the limit or not, as he chooses; and as for the master himself, where is his limit? He may, if he likes, flog a slave to death, for the laws which pretend that he may not are a mere pretense, inasmuch as the testimony of a black is never taken against a white; and upon this plantation of ours, and a thousand more, the overseer is the *only* white man, so whence should come the testimony to any crime of his?

To return to our head driver, or, as he is familiarly called, head man, Frank—he is second in authority only to the overseer, and exercises rule alike over the drivers and the gangs in the absence of the sovereign white man from the estate, which happens whenever Mr. O——visits the other two plantations at Woodville and St. Simon's. He is sole master and governor of the island, appoints the work, pronounces punishments, gives permission to the men to leave the island (without it they never may do so), and exercises all functions of undisputed mastery over his fellow-slaves, for you will observe that all this while he is just as much a slave as any of the rest. Trustworthy, upright, intelligent, he may be flogged to-morrow if Mr. O—— or Mr. Butler so please it, and sold the next day, like a cart-horse, at the will of the latter. Besides his various other responsibilities, he has the key of all the stores, and gives out the people's rations weekly; nor is it only the people's provisions that are put under his charge—meat, which is only given out to them occasionally, and provisions for the use of the family, are also intrusted to his care.

From the imperceptible but inevitable effect of the sympathies and influences of human creatures toward and over each other, Frank's intelligence has become uncommonly developed by intimate communion in the discharge of his duty with the former overseer, a very intelligent man, who has only just left the estate, after managing it for nineteen years; the effect of this intercourse, and of the trust and responsibility laid upon the man, are that he is clear-headed, well judging, active, intelligent, extremely well mannered, and, being respected, he respects himself. He is as ignorant as the rest of the slaves; but he is always clean and tidy in his person, with a courteousness of demeanor far removed from servility, and exhibits a strong instance of the intolerable and wicked injustice of the system under which he lives, having advanced thus far toward improvement, in spite of all the bars it puts to progress; and here being arrested, not by want of energy, want of sense, or any want of his own, but by being held as another man's property, who can only thus hold him by forbidding him farther improvement. When I see that man, who keeps himself a good deal aloof from the rest, in his leisure hours looking, with a countenance of deep thought, as I did today, over the broad river, which is to him as a prison wall, to the fields and forest beyond, not one inch or branch of which his utmost industry can conquer as his own, or acquire and leave an independent heritage to his children, I marvel what the thoughts of such a man may be. I was in his house to-day, and the same superiority in cleanliness, comfort, and propriety exhibited itself in his dwelling as in his own personal appearance and that of his wife —a most active, trustworthy, excellent woman, daughter of the oldest, and probably most highly respected of all Mr. Butler's slaves. To the excellent conduct of this woman, and, indeed, every member of her family, both the present and the last overseer bear unqualified testimony.

As I was returning toward the house after my long morning's lounge, a man rushed out of the blacksmith's shop, and, catching me by the skirt of my gown, poured forth a torrent of self-gratulations on having at length found the "right missis." They have no idea, of course, of a white person performing any of the offices of a servant, and as throughout the whole Southern country the owner's children are nursed and tended, and sometimes *suckled* by their slaves, the appearance of Margery with my two children had immediately suggested the idea that she must be the missis. Many of the poor negroes flocked to her, paying their profound homage under this impression; and when she explained to them that she was not their owner's wife, the confusion in their minds seemed very great—Heaven only knows whether they did not conclude that they had two mistresses, and Mr. Butler two wives! The ecstasy of the blacksmith on discovering the "right missis" at last was very funny, and was expressed with such extraordinary grimaces, contortions, and gesticulations, that I thought I should have died of laughing.

Having at length extricated myself from the group which forms round me whenever I stop but for a few minutes, I pursued my voyage of discovery by peeping into the kitchen garden. A few cabbages and weeds innumerable filled the neglected-looking inclosure, and I ventured no farther than the entrance into its most uninviting precincts. You are to understand that upon this swamp island of ours we have quite a large stock of cattle, cows, sheep, pigs, and poultry in the most enormous and inconvenient abundance. The cows are pretty miserably off for pasture, the banks and pathways of the dikes being their only grazing ground, which the sheep perambulate also, in earnest search of a nibble of fresh herbage; both the cows and sheep are fed with rice flour in great abundance, and are pretty often carried down for change of air and more sufficient grazing to Hampton, Mr. Butler's estate, on the island of St. Simon's, fifteen miles from this place, farther down the river—or rather, indeed, I should say in the sea, for 'tis salt water all round, and one end of the island has a noble beach open to the vast Atlantic. The pigs thrive admirably here, and attain very great perfection of size and flavor, the rice flour upon which they are chiefly fed tending to make them very delicate. As for the poultry, it being one of the few privileges of the poor blacks to raise as many as they can, their abundance is literally a nuisance—ducks, fowls, pigeons, turkeys (the two latter species, by-the-by, are exclusively the master's property), cluck, scream, gabble, gobble, crow, cackle, fight, fly, and flutter in all directions, and to their immense concourse, and the perfect freedom with which they intrude themselves even into the piazza of the house, the pantry, and kitchen, I partly attribute the swarms of fleas, and other still less agreeable vermin, with which we are most horribly pestered.

My walk lay to-day along the bank of a canal, which has been dug through nearly the whole length of the island, to render more direct and easy the transportation of the rice from one end of the estate to another, or from

23

the various distant fields to the principal mill at Settlement No. 1. It is of considerable width and depth, and opens by various locks into the river. I had a conversation that interested me a good deal during my walk with my peculiar slave Jack. This lad, whom Mr. Butler has appointed to attend me in my roamings about the island, and rowing expeditions on the river, is the son of the last head driver, a man of very extraordinary intelligence and faithfulness. In the burial-ground of the negroes is a stone dedicated to his memory, a mark of distinction accorded by his masters, which his son never failed to point out to me when we passed that way. Jack appears to inherit his quickness of apprehension; his questions, like those of an intelligent child, are absolutely inexhaustible; his curiosity about all things beyond this island, the prison-house of his existence, is perfectly intense; his countenance is very pleasing, mild, and not otherwise than thoughtful; he is, in common with the rest of them, a stupendous flatterer, and, like the rest of them, also seems devoid of physical and moral courage.

To-day, in the midst of his torrent of inquiries about places and things, I suddenly asked him if he would like to be free. A gleam of light absolutely shot over his whole countenance, like the vivid and instantaneous lightning; he stammered, hesitated, became excessively confused, and at length replied, "Free, missis! What for me wish to be free? Oh no, missis, me no wish to be free, if massa only let me keep pig!" The fear of offending by uttering that forbidden wish—the dread of admitting, by its expression, the slightest discontent with his present situation—the desire to conciliate my favor, even at the expense of strangling the intense natural longing that absolutely glowed in his every feature—it was a sad spectacle,

24

and I repented my question. As for the pitiful request, which he reiterated several times, adding, "No, missis, me no want to be free; me work till me die for missis and massa," with increased emphasis; it amounted only to this, that negroes once were, but no longer are, permitted to keep pigs. The increase of filth and foul smells consequent upon their being raised is, of course, very great; and, moreover, Mr. Butler told me, when I preferred poor Jack's request to him, that their allowance was no more than would suffice their own necessity, and that they had not the means of feeding the animals.

I told Mr. Butler, with much indignation, of poor Harriet's flogging, and represented that if the people were to be chastised for any thing they said to me, I must leave the place, as I could not but hear their complaints, and endeavor, by all my miserable limited means, to better their condition while I was here. He said he would ask Mr. O—— about it, assuring me, at the same time, that it was impossible to believe a single word any of these people said. At dinner, accordingly, the inquiry was made as to the cause of her punishment, and Mr. O—— then said it was not at all for what she had told me that he had flogged her, but for having answered him impertinently; that he had ordered her into the field, whereupon she had said she was ill and could not work; that he retorted he knew better, and bade her get up and go to work; she replied, "Very well, I'll go, but I shall just come back again!" meaning that when in the field she would be unable to work, and obliged to return to the hospital. "For this reply," Mr. O—— said, "I gave her a good lashing; it was her business to have gone into the field without answering me, and then we should have soon seen whether she could work or not; I gave it to Chloe too for some such impudence." With this sauce I ate my dinner, and truly it tasted bitter.

Toward sunset I went on the river to take my rowing lesson. A darling little canoe, which carries two oars and a steersman, and rejoices in the appropriate title of the "Dolphin," is my especial vessel; and with Jack's help and instructions, I contrived this evening to row upward of half a mile, coasting the reed-crowned edge of the island to another very large rice mill, the enormous wheel of which is turned by the tide. Amphibious creatures, alligators, serpents, and wild-fowl haunt these yet but half-formed regions, where land and water are of the consistency of hasty-pudding—the one seeming too unstable to walk on, the other almost too thick to float in.

At six o'clock our little canoe grazed the steps at the landing. These were covered with young women, and boys, and girls, drawing water for their various household purposes. A very small cedar pail—a piggin as they termed it—serves to scoop up the river water; and having, by this means, filled a large bucket, they transfer this to their heads, and, thus laden, march home. As I ascended the stairs, they surrounded me with shrieks and yells of joy, uttering exclamations of delight and amazement at my rowing. It was only just six o'clock, and these women had all done their tasks. I exhorted them to go home and wash their children, and clean their houses and themselves, which they professed themselves ready to do, but they had no soap. Then began a chorus of mingled requests for soap, for summer clothing, and a variety of things, which, if "Missis only give we, we be so clean forever!"

This request for summer clothing, by-the-by, I think a very reasonable one. The allowance of clothes made yearly to each slave by the present regulations of the estate is a certain number of yards of flannel, and as much more of what they call plains—an extremely stout, thick, heavy woolen cloth, of a dark gray or blue color. This, and two pair of shoes, is the regular ration of clothing; but these plains would be intolerable to any but negroes, even in winter, in this climate, and are intolerable to them in the summer. Disengaging myself from them, for they held my hands and clothes, I conjured them to offer us some encouragement to better their condition by bettering it as much as they could themselves—enforced the virtue of washing themselves and all belonging to them, and at length made good my retreat.

THE DOCTOR & DARIEN

JANUARY 1839

WE HAD A SPECIES of fish this morning for our breakfast which deserves more glory than I can bestow upon
it. I took a long walk this morning to Settlement No. 3,
the third village on the island. My way lay along the
side of the canal, beyond which, and only divided from
it by a raised narrow causeway, rolled the brimming
river, with its girdle of glittering evergreens, while on my
other hand a deep trench marked the line of the rice fields.
I visited the people and houses here. I found nothing in
any respect different from what I have described to you
at Settlement No. 1.

In the afternoon I and Jack rowed ourselves over to
Darien. It is Saturday—the day of the week on which
the slaves from the island are permitted to come over to
the town to purchase such things as they may require and
can afford, and to dispose, to the best advantage, of their
poultry, moss, and eggs. I met many of them paddling
themselves singly in their slight canoes, scooped out of
the trunk of a tree, and parties of three and four rowing
boats of their own building, laden with their purchases,
singing, laughing, talking, and apparently enjoying their

holiday to the utmost. They all hailed me with shouts of delight as I pulled past them, and many were the injunctions bawled after Jack to "mind and take good care of missis!" We returned home through the glory of a sunset all amber-colored and rosy, and found that one of the slaves, a young lad for whom Mr. Butler has a particular regard, was dangerously ill. Dr. Holmes was sent for; and there is every probability that he, Mr. Butler, and Mr. O—— will be up all night with the poor fellow.

To-day being Sunday, a large boat full of Mr. Butler's people from Hampton came up, to go to church at Darien, and to pay their respects to their master, and see their new "missis." The same scene was acted over again that occurred on our first arrival. A crowd clustered round the house door, to whom I and my babies were produced, and with every individual of whom we had to shake hands some half a dozen times. They brought us up presents of eggs (their only wealth), beseeching us to take them; and one young lad, the son of head man Frank, had a beautiful pair of chickens, which he offered most earnestly to Sally. We took one of them, not to mortify the poor fellow, and a green ribbon being tied round its leg, it became a sacred fowl, "little missis's chicken." The expressions of devotion and delight of these poor people are the most fervent you can imagine. One of them, speaking to me of Mr. Butler, and saying that they had heard that he had not been well, added, "Oh! We hear so, missis, and we not know what to do. Oh! Missis, massa sick, all him people *broken*!"

Dr. Holmes came again to-day to see the poor sick boy, who is doing much better, and bidding fair to recover. He entertained me with an account of the Darien society, its aristocracies and democracies, its little grandeurs and smaller pettinesses, its circles higher and lower, its social jealousies, fine invisible lines of demarkation, imperceptible shades of different respectability, and delicate divisions of genteel, genteeler, genteelest. He is a shrewd, intelligent man, with an excellent knowledge of his profession, much kindness of heart, and apparent cheerful good temper. I have already severely tried the latter by the unequivocal expression of my opinions on the subject of slavery, and, though I perceived that it required all his self-command to listen with any thing like patience to my highly incendiary and inflammatory doctrines, he yet did so, and though he was, I have no doubt, perfectly horror-stricken at the discovery, lost nothing of his courtesy or good-humor. By-the-by, I must tell you that, at an early period of the conversation, upon my saying, "I put all other considerations out of the question, and first propose to you the injustice of the system alone," "Oh," replied my friend the doctor, "if you put it upon that ground, you *stump* the question at once; I have nothing to say to that whatever, but," and then followed the usual train of pleadings—happiness, tenderness, care, indulgence, etc., etc., etc.—all the substitutes that may or may not be put in the place of *justice*, and which these slaveholders attempt to persuade others, and perhaps themselves, effectually supply its want.

After church hours the people came back from Darien. They are only permitted to go to Darien to church once a month. On the intermediate Sundays they assemble in the house of London, Mr. Butler's head cooper, an excellent and pious man, who has obtained some little knowledge of reading, and who reads prayers and the Bible to his fellow-slaves, and addresses them with extemporaneous exhortations. At Darien a church is appropriated to the especial use of the slaves, who are almost all of them Baptists here; and a gentleman officiates in it (of course white), who, I understand, is very zealous in the cause of their spiritual well-being. He, like most Southern men, clergy or others, jump the present life in their charities to the slaves, and go on to furnish them with all requisite conveniences for the next. There were a short time ago two free black preachers in this neighborhood, but they have lately been ejected from the place.

You can not conceive any thing more grotesque than the Sunday trim of the poor people. Their Sabbath toilet really presents the most ludicrous combination of incongruities that you can conceive—frills, flounces, ribbons; combs stuck in their woolly heads, as if they held up any portion of the stiff and ungovernable hair; filthy finery, every color in the rainbow, and the deepest possible shades blended in fierce companionship round one dusky visage; head-handkerchiefs, that put one's very eyes out from a mile off; chintzes with sprawling patterns, that might be seen if the clouds were printed with them; beads, bugles, flaring sashes, and, above all, little fanciful aprons, which finish these incongruous toilets with a sort of airy grace, which I assure you is perfectly indescribable. One young man, the eldest son and heir of our washerwoman Hannah, came to pay his respects to me in a magnificent black satin waistcoat, shirt gills which absolutely ingulfed his black visage, and neither shoes nor stockings on his feet.

Among our visitors from St. Simon's to-day was Hannah's mother (it seems to me that there is not a girl of sixteen on the plantations but has children, nor a woman of thirty but has grandchildren). Old House Molly, as she is called, from the circumstance of her having been one of the slaves employed in domestic offices during Major Butler's residence on the island, is one of the oldest and most respected slaves on the estate, and was introduced to me by Mr. Butler with especial marks of attention and regard; she absolutely embraced him, and seemed unable sufficiently to express her ecstasy at seeing him again. Her dress, like that of her daughter, and all the servants who have at any time been employed about the family, bore witness to a far more improved taste than the half savage adornment of the other poor blacks, and upon my observing to her how agreeable her neat and cleanly appearance was to me, she replied that her old master (Major Butler) was extremely particular in this respect, and that in his time all the house servants were obliged to be very nice and careful about their persons. She named to me all her children, an immense tribe.

On Monday evening I rowed over to Darien with Mr. Butler to fetch over the doctor, who was coming to visit some of our people. As I sat waiting in the boat for the return of the gentlemen, the sun went down, or rather seemed to dissolve bodily into the glowing clouds, which appeared but a fusion of the great orb of light; the stars twinkled out in the rose-colored sky, and the evening air, as it fanned the earth to sleep, was as soft as a summer's evening breeze in the north. A sort of dreamy stillness seemed creeping over the world and into my spirit as the canoe just tilted against the steps that led to the wharf, raised by the scarce perceptible heaving of the water. A melancholy, monotonous boat-horn sounded from a distance up the stream, and presently, floating slowly down with the current, huge, shapeless, black, relieved against the sky, came one of those rough barges piled with cotton, called, hereabouts, Oconee boxes. The vessel itself is really nothing but a monstrous square box, made of rough planks, put together in the roughest manner possible to attain the necessary object of keeping the cotton dry. Upon this great tray are piled the swollen cotton-bags, to the height of ten, twelve, and fourteen feet. This huge water-wagon floats lazily down the river, from the upper country to Darien. They are flat-bottomed, and, of course, draw little water. The stream from whence they are named is an up-country river, which, by its junction with the Ocmulgee, forms the Altamaha. These Oconee boxes are broken up at Darien, where the cotton is shipped either for the Savannah, Charleston, or Liverpool markets, and the timber of which they are constructed sold.

I went again to-day to the Infirmary, and was happy to perceive that there really was an evident desire to conform to my instructions, and keep the place in a better condition than formerly. Among the sick I found a poor woman suffering dreadfully from the ear ache. She had done nothing to alleviate her pain but apply some leaves, of what tree or plant I could not ascertain, and tie up her head in a variety of dirty cloths, till it was as large as her whole body. I removed all these, and found one side of her face and neck very much swollen, but so begrimed with filth that it was really no very agreeable task to examine it. The first process, of course, was washing, which, however, appeared to her so very unusual an operation, that I had to perform it for her myself. Sweet oil and laudanum, and raw cotton, being then applied to her ear and neck, she professed herself much relieved.

My next office in the Infirmary this morning was

superintending the washing of two little babies, whose mothers were nursing them with quite as much ignorance as zeal. Having ordered a large tub of water, I desired Rose to undress the little creatures and give them a warm bath; the mothers looked on in unutterable dismay; and one of them, just as her child was going to be put into the tub, threw into it all the clothes she had just taken off it, as she said, to break the unusual shock of the warm water. I immediately rescued them; not but what they were quite as much in want of washing as the baby, but it appeared, upon inquiry, that the woman had none others to dress the child in when it should have taken its bath; they were immediately wrung and hung by the fire to dry; and the poor little patients, having undergone this novel operation, were taken out and given to their mothers. Any thing, however, much more helpless and inefficient than these poor ignorant creatures you can not conceive; they actually seemed incapable of drying or dressing their own babies, and I had to finish their toilet myself. In the next room I found a woman lying on the floor in a fit of epilepsy, barking most violently. She seemed to excite no particular attention or compassion; the women said she was subject to these fits, and took little or no notice of her, as she lay barking like some enraged animal on the ground.

Returning to the house, I passed up the "street." It was between eleven o'clock and noon, and the people were taking their first meal in the day. They go to the fields at daybreak, carrying with them their allowance of food for the day, which toward noon, *and not till then*, they eat, cooking it over a fire, which they kindle as best they can, where they are working. Their second meal in the day is at night, after their labor is over, having worked, at the *very least*, six hours without intermission of rest or refreshment since their noonday meal (properly so called, for 'tis meal, and nothing else). Those that I passed to-day, sitting on their door-steps, or on the ground round them eating, were the people employed at the mill and threshing-floor. As these are near to the settlement, they had time to get their food from the cook-shop. Chairs, tables, plates, knives, forks, they had none; they sat, as I before said, on the earth or door-steps, and ate either out of their little cedar tubs or an iron pot, some few with broken iron spoons, more with pieces of wood, and all the children with their fingers.

At one of the doors I saw three young girls standing, who might be between sixteen and seventeen years old; they had evidently done eating, and were rudely playing and romping with each other, laughing and shouting like wild things. I went into the house, and such another spectacle of filthy disorder I never beheld. I then addressed the girls most solemnly, showing them that they were wasting in idle riot the time in which they might be rendering their abode decent, and told them that it was a shame for any woman to live in so dirty a place and so beastly a condition. They said they had seen buckree (white) women's houses just as dirty, and they could not be expected to be cleaner than white women. I then told them that the only difference between themselves and buckree women was, that the latter were generally better informed, and for that reason alone, it was more disgraceful for them to be disorderly and dirty. They seemed to listen to me attentively, and one of them exclaimed, with great satisfaction, that they saw I made no difference between them and white girls, and that they never had been so treated before. You see them, boys and girls, from the youngest age to seventeen and eighteen, rolling, tumbling, kicking, and wallowing in the dust, regardless alike of decency, and incapable of any more rational amusement; or lolling, with half-closed eyes, like so many cats and dogs, against a wall, or upon a bank in the sun, dozing away their short leisure hour, until called to resume their labors in the field or the mill.

After this description of the meals of our laborers, you will, perhaps, be curious to know how it fares with our house servants in this respect. Precisely in the same manner, as far as regards allowance, with the exception of what is left from our table, but, if possible, with even less comfort, in one respect, inasmuch as no time whatever is set apart for their meals, which they snatch at any hour, and in any way that they can—generally, however, standing, or squatting on their hams round the kitchen fire. They have no sleeping-rooms in the house, but when their work is over, retire, like the rest, to their hovels, the discomfort of which has to them all the addition of comparison with our mode of living. The young woman who performs the office of lady's-maid, and the lads who wait upon us at table, have neither table to feed nor chair to sit down upon themselves. The boys sleep at night on the hearth by the kitchen fire, and the women upon a rough board bedstead, strewed with a little tree moss.

I am amusing myself by attempting to beautify, in some sort, this residence of ours. Immediately at the back of it runs a ditch, about three feet wide, which empties and fills twice a day with the tide. This lies like a moat on two sides of the house. The opposite bank is a steep dike, with a footpath along the top. One or two willows droop over this very interesting ditch, and I thought I would add to their company some magnolias and myrtles, so as to make a little evergreen plantation round the house. I went to the swamp reserves I have before mentioned to you, and chose some beautiful bushes—among others, a very fine young pine, at which our overseer and all the negroes expressed much contemptuous surprise; for, though the tree is beautiful, it is also common, and with them, as with wiser folk, 'tis "nothing pleases but rare accidents." In spite of their disparaging remarks, however, I persisted in having my pine-tree planted, and I assure you it formed a very pleasing variety among the broad, smooth-leaved evergreens about it. Having worked my appointed task in the garden, I rowed over to Darien and back, the rosy sunset changing mean time to starry evening, as beautiful as the first the sky ever was arrayed in.

MR. KING

JANUARY 1839

AFTER FINISHING my last letter, I went out into the clear starlight to breathe the delicious mildness of the air, and was surprised to hear rising from one of the houses of the settlement a hymn sung apparently by a number of voices. The next morning I inquired the meaning of this, and was informed that those negroes on the planta-tion who were members of the Church were holding a prayer-meeting. There is an immensely strong devotional feeling among these poor people. Some of the planters are entirely inimical to any such proceedings, and neither allow their negroes to attend worship, or to congregate together for religious purposes. On other plantations, again, the same rigid discipline is not observed; and some planters and overseers go even farther than toleration, and encourage these devotional exercises and professions of religion, having actually discovered that a man may become more faithful and trustworthy, even as a slave, who acknowledges the higher influences of Christianity, no matter in how small a degree. Slaveholding clergy-men, and certain piously inclined planters, undertake, accordingly, to enlighten these poor creatures upon these matters, with a safe understanding, however, of what truth is to be given to them, and what is not; how much they may learn to become better slaves, and how much they may not learn, lest they cease to be slaves at all.

I really never was so busy in all my life as I am here. From morning till night, no time, no place affords me a respite from my innumerable petitioners; and whether I be asleep or awake, reading, eating, or walking—in the kitchen, my bedroom, or the parlor, they flock in with urgent entreaties and pitiful stories, and my conscience forbids my ever postponing their business for any other matter; for, with shame and grief of heart I say it, by their unpaid labor I live—their nakedness clothes me, and their heavy toil maintains me in luxurious idleness.

Mr. Butler has been much gratified to-day by the arrival of Mr. King, who, with his father, for nineteen years was the sole manager of these estates, and discharged his laborious task with great ability and fidelity toward his employers. How far he understood his duties to the slaves, or whether, indeed, an overseer can, in the nature of things, acknowledge any duty to them, is another question. He is a remarkable man, and is much respected for his integrity and honorable dealing by every body here. His activity and energy are wonderful; and the mere fact of his having charge of for nineteen years, and personally governing, without any assistance whatever, seven hundred people scattered over three large tracts of land, at a considerable distance from each other, certainly bespeaks efficiency and energy of a very uncommon order. The character I had heard of him from Mr. Butler had excited a great deal of interest in me, and I was very glad of this opportunity of seeing a man who for so many years had been sovereign over the poor people here. I met him walking on the banks with Mr. Butler as I returned from my own ramble. My companions, when I do not request the attendance of my friend Jack, are a couple of little terriers.

I crossed the threshing-floor to-day—a very large square, perfectly level, raised by artificial means about half a foot from the ground, and covered equally all over, so as to lie quite smooth, with some preparation of tar. It lies immediately between the house and the steam mill, and on it much of the negroes' work is done —the first threshing is given to the rice, and other labors are carried on. As I walked across it to-day, passing through the busy groups, chiefly of women, that covered it, I came opposite to one of the drivers, who held in his hand his whip, the odious insignia of his office. I took it from him; it was a short stick of moderate size, with a thick square leather thong attached to it. As I held it in my hand, I did not utter a word; but my face spoke what my tongue did not, for the driver said, "Oh, missis, me use it for measure; me seldom strike nigger with it." For one moment I thought I must carry the hateful implement into the house with me. An instant's reflection, however, served to show me how useless such a proceeding would be. The people are not mine, nor their drivers, nor their whips.

After dinner I had a most interesting conversation with Mr. King. Among other subjects, he gave me a lively and curious description of the pine-landers of Georgia. Have you visions now of well-to-do farmers with comfortable homesteads, decent habits, industrious, intelligent, cheerful, and thrifty? Such, however, is not the yeomanry of Georgia. Labor being here the especial portion of slaves, it is thenceforth degraded, and considered unworthy of all but slaves. No white man, therefore, of any class puts hand to work of any kind soever. I speak now of the scattered white population, who, too poor to possess land or slaves, and having no means of living in the towns, squat either on other men's land or government districts—always here swamp or pine barren—and claim the place they invade till ejected by the rightful proprietors. These wretched creatures will not, for they are whites (and labor belongs to blacks and slaves alone here), labor for their own subsistence. They are hardly protected from the weather by the rude shelters they frame for themselves in the midst of these dreary woods. Their food is chiefly supplied by shooting the wild-fowl and venison, and stealing from the cultivated patches of the plantations nearest at hand. Their clothes hang about them in filthy tatters, and the combined squalor and fierceness of their appearance is really frightful. This population is the direct growth of slavery. The planters are loud in their execrations of these miserable vagabonds.

THE RICE MILL

JANUARY 1839

SINCE I LAST WROTE I have been called upon by several families residing in and about Darien, and rowed over in due form to acknowledge the honor. How shall I describe Darien to you? Half buried in sand, its straggling, tumble-down wooden houses peer over the muddy bank of the thick slimy river. The whole town lies in a bed of sand: side-walks, or mid-walks, there be none distinct from each other; at every step I took my feet were ankle deep in the soil, and I had cause to rejoice that I was booted for the occasion. Our worthy doctor, whose lady I was going to visit, did nothing but regret that I had not allowed him to provide me a carriage, though the distance between his house and the landing is not a quarter of a mile. The houses seemed scattered about here and there, apparently without any design, and looked, for the most part, either unfinished or ruinous. The magnificent oaks seemed to add to the meanness and insignificance of the human dwellings they overshadowed by their enormous size and grotesque forms. Our doctor's wife is a New England woman; how can she live here? She gave me some violets and narcissus, already blossoming profusely—in January—and expressed, like her husband, a thousand regrets at my having walked so far.

I have been over the rice mill, under the guidance of the overseer and head man Frank, and have been made acquainted with the whole process of threshing the rice, which is extremely curious. The number of hands employed in this threshing mill is very considerable, and the whole establishment, comprising the fires, and boilers, and machinery of a powerful steam-engine, are all under negro superintendence and direction. After this survey I occupied myself with my infant plantation of evergreens round the dike, in the midst of which interesting pursuit I was interrupted by a visit from Mr. Barrett, a neighboring planter, who came to transact some business with Mr. Butler about rice which he had sent to our mill to have threshed, and the price to be paid for such threshing. The negroes have presented a petition to-day that they may be allowed to have a ball in honor of our arrival, which demand has been acceded to, and furious preparations are being set on foot.

THE OLD CRONE

JANUARY 1839

I RECEIVED early this morning a visit from a young negro called Morris, who came to request permission to be baptized. The master's leave is necessary for this ceremony of acceptance into the bosom of the Christian Church. I have seldom seen a more pleasing appearance than that of this young man; his figure was tall and straight, and his face, which was of a perfect oval, rejoiced in the grace, very unusual among his people, of a fine high forehead, and the much more frequent one of a remarkably gentle and sweet expression. There is a certain African tribe from which the West Indian slave-market is chiefly recruited, who have these same characteristic features, and do not at all present the ignoble and ugly negro type, so much more commonly seen here. They are a tall, powerful people, with remarkably fine figures, regular features, and a singularly warlike and fierce disposition, in which respect they also differ from the race of negroes existing on the American plantations.

On their return from their walk this afternoon the children brought home some pieces of sugar-cane, of which a small quantity grows on the island. It is a long green reed, like the stalk of the maize, or Indian corn, only it shoots up to a much more considerable height, and has a consistent pith, which, together with the rind itself, is extremely sweet. The principal peculiarity of this growth, as perhaps you know, is that they are laid horizontally in the earth when they are planted for propagation, and from each of the notches or joints of the recumbent cane a young shoot is produced at the germinating season.

I have been walking to another cluster of negro huts, known as Number Two, and here we took a boat and rowed across the broad brimming Altamaha to a place called Woodville, on a part of the estate named Hammersmith. This settlement is on the main land, and consists apparently merely of a lonely plank house in the midst of the pine woods (to which the overseer retires when the poisonous malaria of the rice plantations compels him to withdraw from it), and a few deplorably miserable hovels, which appeared to me to be chiefly occupied by the most decrepid and infirm samples of humanity it was ever my melancholy lot to behold.

The air of this pine barren is salubrious compared with that of the rice islands, and here some of the oldest slaves who will not die yet, and can not work any more, are sent. Remote recollections of former dealings with civilized human beings in the shape of masters and overseers seemed to me to be the only idea not purely idiotic in the minds of the poor old tottering creatures that gathered to stare with dim and blear eyes at me and my children.

There were two very aged women, who had seen different, and, to their faded recollections, better times, who spoke to me of Mr. Butler's grandfather, and of the early days of the plantation, when they were young and strong, and worked as their children and grandchildren were now working, neither for love nor yet for money. One of these old crones, a hideous, withered, wrinkled piece of womanhood, said that she had worked as long as her strength had lasted, and that then she had still been worth her keep, for, said she, "Missus, tho' we no able to work, we make little niggers for massa." Her joy at seeing her present owner was unbounded, and she kept clapping her horny hands together and exclaiming, "While there is life there is hope; we seen massa before we die." These demonstrations of regard were followed up by piteous complaints of hunger and rheumatism, and their usual requests for pittances of food and clothing, to which we responded by promises of additions in both kinds.

I was extricating myself as well as I could from my petitioners, with the assurance that I would come by-and-by and visit them again, when I felt my dress suddenly feebly jerked, and a shrill cracked voice on the other side of me exclaimed, "Missus, no go yet—no go away yet; you no see me, missus, when you come by-and-by; but," added the voice, in a sort of wail, which seemed to me as if the thought was full of misery, "you see many, many of my offspring." These melancholy words, particularly the rather unusual one at the end of the address, struck me very much. They were uttered by a creature which *was* a woman, but *looked* like a crooked, ill-built figure set up in a field to scare crows, with a face infinitely more like a mere animal's than any human countenance I ever beheld, and with a peculiar, wild, restless look of indefinite and, at the same time, intense sadness. It was almost with an effort that I commanded myself so as not to withdraw my dress from the yellow, crumpled, filthy claws that gripped it, and it was not at last without the authoritative voice of the overseer that the poor creature released her hold of me.

We returned home certainly in the very strangest vehicle that ever civilized gentlewoman traveled in—a huge sort of cart, made only of some loose boards, on which I lay, supporting myself against one of the four posts which indicated the sides of my carriage; six horned creatures, cows or bulls, drew this singular equipage, and a yelping, howling, screaming, leaping company of half-naked negroes ran all round them, goading them with sharp sticks, frantically seizing hold of their tails, and inciting them by every conceivable and inconceivable encouragement to quick motion: thus I was dragged through the deep sand from the settlement back to the river, where we re-embarked for the island.

I have had several women at the house to-day asking for advice and help for their sick children: they all came from No. 2, as they call it, that is, the settlement or cluster of negro huts nearest to the main one, where we may be said to reside. In the afternoon I went thither, and found a great many of the little children ailing: there had been an unusual mortality among them at this particular settlement this winter. In one miserable hut I heard that the baby was just dead; it was one of thirteen, many of whom had been, like itself, mercifully removed from the life of degradation and misery to which their birth appointed them; and whether it was the frequent repetition of similar losses, or an instinctive consciousness that death was indeed better than life for such children as theirs, I know not, but the father and mother, and old Rose, the nurse, who was their little baby's grandmother, all seemed apathetic, and apparently indifferent to the event. The mother merely repeated over and over again, "I've lost a many; they all goes so;" and the father, without word or comment, went out to his enforced labor.

As I left the cabin, I found myself suddenly surrounded by a swarm of young ragamuffins in every stage of partial nudity, clamoring from out of their filthy remnants of rags for donations of scarlet ribbon for the ball, which was to take place that evening. At our own settlement (No. 1) I found every thing in a high fever of preparation for the ball. A huge boat had just arrived from the cotton plantation at St. Simon's, laden with the youth and beauty of that portion of the estate who had been invited to join the party; and the greetings among the arrivers and welcomers, and the heaven-defying combinations of color in the gala attire of both, surpass all my powers of description. The ball, to which of course we went, took place in one of the rooms of the Infirmary. As the room had, fortunately, but few occupants, they were removed to another apartment. The dancing commenced. It is impossible for words to describe the things these people did with their bodies, and, above all, with their faces, the whites of their eyes, and the whites of their teeth. The languishing elegance of some—the painstaking laboriousness of others—above all, the feats of a certain enthusiastic banjo-player, who seemed to me to thump his instrument with every part of his body at once, at last utterly overcame any attempt at decorous gravity on my part.

PSYCHE'S SADNESS

JANUARY 1839

I WILL TELL YOU a story which has just formed an admirable illustration for my observation of all the miseries of which this accursed system of slavery is the cause, even under the best and most humane administration of its laws and usages. You will find, in the absence of all voluntary or even conscious cruelty on the part of the master, the best possible comment on a state of things which, without the slightest desire to injure and oppress, produces such intolerable injury and oppression.

We have, as a sort of under nursemaid and assistant, a young woman named Psyche, commonly called Sack; she can not be much over twenty, has a very pretty figure, a graceful, gentle deportment, and a face which, but for its color (she is a dingy mulatto), would be pretty, and is extremely pleasing, from the perfect sweetness of its expression; she is always serious, not to say sad and silent, and has always an air of melancholy and timidity. Just in proportion as I have found the slaves on this plantation intelligent and advanced beyond the general brutish level of the majority, I have observed this pathetic expression of countenance in them, a mixture of sadness

49

and fear, the involuntary exhibition of the two feelings, which I suppose must be the predominant experience of their whole lives, regret and apprehension, not the less heavy, either of them, for being, in some degree, vague and indefinite—a sense of incalculable past loss and injury, and a dread of incalculable future loss and injury.

I have never questioned Psyche as to her sadness. To my great astonishment, the other day Margery asked me if I knew to whom Psyche belonged, as the poor woman had inquired of her with much hesitation and anguish if she could tell her who owned her and her children. She has two nice little children under six years old, whom she keeps as clean and tidy, and who are sad and as silent as herself. My astonishment at this question was, as you will readily believe, not small, and I forthwith sought out Psyche for an explanation. She was thrown into extreme perturbation at finding that her question had been referred to me, and it was some time before I could sufficiently reassure her to be able to comprehend, in the midst of her reiterated entreaties for pardon, and hopes that she had not offended me, that she did not know herself who owned her. She was, at one time, the property of Mr. King, the former overseer, of whom I have already spoken to you, and who has just been paying Mr. Butler a visit. Whether she still belonged to Mr. King or not she did not know, and entreated me, if she did, to endeavor to persuade Mr. Butler to buy her. Now you must know that this poor woman is the wife of one of Mr. Butler's slaves, a fine, intelligent, active, excellent young man, whose whole family are among some of the very best specimens of character and capacity on the estate. I was so astonished at the (to me) extraordinary state of things revealed by poor Sack's petition, that I could only tell her that I had supposed all the negroes on the plantation were Mr. Butler's property, but that I would certainly inquire, and find out for her, if I could, to whom she belonged, and if I could, endeavor to get Mr. Butler to purchase her, if she really was not his.

I did not see Mr. Butler until the evening; but, in the mean time, meeting Mr. O——, the overseer, with whom, as I believe I have already told you, we are living here, I asked him about Psyche, and who was her proprietor, when, to my infinite surprise, he told me that *he* had bought her and her children from Mr. King, who had offered them to him, saying that they would be rather troublesome to him where he was going; "and so," said Mr. O——, "as I had no objection to investing a little money that way, I bought them." With a heart much lightened, I flew to tell poor Psyche the news, so that, at any rate, she might be relieved from the dread of any immediate separation from her husband. You can imagine better than I can tell you what her sensations were; but she still renewed her prayer that I would, if possible, induce Mr. Butler to purchase her, and I promised to do so.

Early the next morning, while I was still dressing, I was suddenly startled by hearing voices in loud tones in Mr. Butler's dressing-room, which adjoins my bedroom, and the noise increasing until there was an absolute cry of despair uttered by some man. I could restrain myself no longer, but opened the door of communication and saw Joe, the young man, poor Psyche's husband, raving almost in a state of frenzy, and in a voice broken with sobs and almost inarticulate with passion, reiterating his determination never to leave this plantation, never to go to Alabama, never to leave his old father and mother, his poor wife and children, and dashing his hat, which he was wringing like a cloth in his hands, upon the ground, he declared he would kill himself if he was compelled to follow Mr. King. I glanced from the poor wretch to Mr. Butler, who was standing, leaning against a table with his arms folded, occasionally uttering a few words of counsel to his slave to be quiet and not fret, and not make a fuss about what there was no help for. I retreated immediately from the horrid scene, breathless with surprise and dismay, and stood for some time in my own room, with my heart and temples throbbing to such a degree that I could hardly support myself. As soon as I recovered myself I again sought Mr. O——, and inquired of him if he knew the cause of poor Joe's distress. He then told me that Mr. Butler, who is highly pleased with Mr. King's past administration of his property, wished, on his departure for his newly-acquired slave plantation, to give him some token of his satisfaction, and *had made him a present* of the man Joe, who had just received the intelligence that he was to go down to Alabama with his new owner the next day, leaving father, mother, wife, and children behind.

When I saw Mr. Butler after this most wretched story became known to me in all its details, I appealed to him not to commit so great a cruelty. How I cried, and how I adjured, and how all my sense of justice, and of mercy, and of pity for the poor wretch, and of wretchedness at finding myself implicated in such a state of things, broke in torrents of words from my lips and tears from my eyes! Mr. Butler gave me no answer whatever, and I have since thought that the intemperate vehemence of my entreaties and expostulations perhaps deserved that he should leave me as he did without one single word of reply; and miserable enough I remained.

Toward evening, as I was sitting alone, my children having gone to bed, Mr. O—— came into the room. I had but one subject in my mind; I had not been able to eat for it. I could hardly sit still for the nervous distress which every thought of these poor people filled me with. As he sat down looking over some accounts, I said to him, "Have you seen Joe this afternoon, Mr. O——?" "Yes, ma'am; he is a great deal happier than he was this morning." "Why, how is that?" asked I, eagerly. "Oh, he is not going to Alabama. Mr. King heard that he had kicked up a fuss about it, and said that if the fellow wasn't willing to go with him, he did not wish to be bothered with any niggers down there who were to be troublesome, so he might stay behind." "And does Psyche know this?" "Yes, ma'am, I suppose so." I drew a long breath. The man was for the present safe, and I remained silently pondering his deliverance and the whole proceeding, and the conduct of every one engaged in it, and, above all, Mr. Butler's share in the transaction, and I think, for the first time, almost a sense of horrible personal responsibility and implication took hold of my mind, and I felt the weight of an unimagined guilt upon my conscience.

With these agreeable reflections I went to bed. Mr. Butler said not a word to me upon the subject of these poor people all the next day, and in the mean time I became very impatient of this reserve on his part, because I was dying to prefer my request that he would purchase Psyche and her children, and so prevent any future separation between her and her husband, as I supposed he would not again attempt to make a present of Joe. In the evening I was again with Mr. O—— alone in the strange, bare, wooden-walled sort of shanty which is our sitting-room, and revolving in my mind the means of rescuing Psyche from her miserable suspense. I suddenly accosted Mr. O——, it was to this effect: "Mr. O——, I have a particular favor to beg of you. Promise me that you will never sell Psyche and her children without first letting me know of your intention to do so, and giving me the option of buying them." Mr. O—— laid down a book he was reading, and directed his head and one of his eyes toward me and answered, "Dear me, ma'am, I am very sorry—I have sold them." My work fell down on the ground, and my mouth opened wide, but I could utter no sound, I was so dismayed and surprised; and he deliberately proceeded: "I didn't know, ma'am, you see, at all, that *you* entertained any idea of making an investment of that nature; for I'm sure, if I had, I would willingly have sold the woman to you; but I sold her and her children this morning to *Mr.* Butler." I jumped up and left Mr. O—— still speaking, and ran to find Mr. Butler, to thank him for what he had done. Think how it fares with slaves on plantations where there is no crazy English woman to weep, and entreat, and implore, and upbraid for them, and no master willing to listen to such appeals.

SHADRACH'S FUNERAL

JANUARY 1839

ROWING YESTERDAY EVENING through a beautiful sunset into a more beautiful moonrise, my two sable boatmen entertained themselves and me with alternate strophe and antistrophe of poetical description of my personal attractions, in which my "wire waist" recurred repeatedly, to my intense amusement. This is a charm for the possession of which Margery (my white nursemaid) is also invariably celebrated. Occasionally I am celebrated in these rowing chants as "Massa's darling," and Sally comes in for endless glorification on account of the brilliant beauty of her complexion.

Yesterday morning I amused myself with an exercise of a talent I once possessed, but have so neglected that my performance might almost be called an experiment. I cut out a dress for one of the women. Tall, large, straight, well made, profoundly serious, she stood like a bronze statue, while I, mounted on a stool (the only way in which I could attain to the noble shoulders and bust of my lay figure), pinned and measured, and cut and shaped, under the superintendence of Margery, and had the satisfaction of seeing the fine proportions of my black

55

goddess quite becomingly clothed in a high, tight-fitting body of the gayest chintz, which she really contrived to put together quite creditably.

I was so elated with my own part of this performance that I then and there determined to put into execution a plan I had long formed of endowing the little boat in which I take what the French call my walks on the water with cushions for the back and seat of the benches usually occupied by myself and Mr. Butler; so, putting on my large straw hat, and plucking up a paper of pins, scissors, and my brown holland, I walked to the steps, and, jumping into the little canoe, began piecing, and measuring, and cutting the cushions, which were to be stuffed with the tree moss by some of the people who understand making a rough kind of mattress. My inanimate subject, however, proved far more troublesome to fit than my living lay figure, for the little cockle-shell ducked, and dived, and rocked, and tipped, and courtesied, and tilted, as I knelt first on one side and then on the other, fitting her, till I was almost in despair; however, I got a sort of pattern at last, and the little Dolphin rejoiced in very tidy back and seat cushions, covered with brown holland, and bound with green serge.

We have had a death among the people since I last wrote to you. A very valuable slave called Shadrach was seized with a disease which is frequent, and very apt to be fatal here—peripneumonia; and, in spite of all that could be done to save him, sank rapidly, and died after an acute illness of only three days. The doctor came repeatedly from Darien, and the last night of the poor fellow's life Mr. Butler himself watched with him.

Yesterday evening the burial of poor Shadrach took place. I had been applied to for a sufficient quantity of cotton cloth to make a winding-sheet for him, and just as the twilight was thickening into darkness I went with Mr. Butler to the cottage of one of the slaves, a cooper by the name of London, the head of the religious party of the inhabitants of the island, a Methodist preacher of no small intelligence and influence among the people—who was to perform the burial service. The coffin was laid on trestles in front of the cooper's cottage, and a large assemblage of the people had gathered round, many of the men carrying pine-wood torches, the fitful glare of which glanced over the strange assembly.

Presently the whole congregation uplighted their voices in a hymn, the first high wailing notes of which —sung all in unison, in the midst of these unwonted surroundings—sent a thrill through all my nerves. When the chant ceased, Cooper London began a prayer, and all the people knelt down in the sand, as I did also. Mr. Butler alone remained standing in the presence of the dead man and of the living God to whom his slaves were now appealing. When the prayer was concluded we all rose, and, the coffin being taken up, proceeded to the people's burial-ground, when London read aloud portions of the funeral service from the Prayer-book. There was something painful to me in Mr. Butler's standing while we all knelt on the earth; for, though in any church in Philadelphia he would have stood during the prayer of any minister, here I wished he would have knelt, to have given his slaves some token of his belief that—at least in the sight of that Master to whom we were addressing our worship—all men are equal. The service ended with a short address from London upon the subject of Lazarus, and the confirmation which the story of his resurrection afforded our hopes.

When the coffin was lowered the grave was found to be partially filled with water—naturally enough, for the whole island is a mere swamp, off which the Altamaha is only kept from sweeping by the high dikes all round it. This seemed to shock and distress the people, and for the first time during the whole ceremony there were sounds of crying and exclamations of grief heard among them. Their chief expression of sorrow, however, when Mr. Butler and myself bade them good-night at the conclusion of the service, was on account of my crying, which appeared to affect them very much, many of them mingling with their "Farewell, good-night, massa and missis," affectionate exclamations of "God bless you, missis; don't cry!" "Lor, missis, don't you cry so!" Mr. Butler declined the assistance of any of the torch-bearers home, and bade them all go quietly to their quarters; and as soon as they had dispersed, and we had got beyond the fitful and unequal glaring of the torches, we found the shining of the stars in the deep blue lovely night sky quite sufficient to light our way along the dikes. I could not speak to Mr. Butler, but continued to cry as we walked silently home.

HOSPITAL VISITS

FEBRUARY 1839

RETURNING FROM THE HOSPITAL, I was accosted by poor old Teresa, the wretched negress who had complained to me so grievously of her back being broken by hard work and childbearing. She was in a dreadful state of excitement, which she partly presently communicated to me, because she said Mr. O—— had ordered her to be flogged for having complained to me as she did. Punishing these wretched creatures for crying out to me for help is really converting me into a source of increased misery to them. It is almost more than I can endure to hear these horrid stories of lashings inflicted because I have been invoked; and though I dare say Mr. Butler, thanks to my passionate appeals to him, gives me little credit for prudence or self-command, I have some, and I exercise it, too, when I listen to such tales as these with my teeth set fast and my lips closed. Whatever I may do to the master, I hold my tongue to the slaves, and I wonder how I do it.

In the afternoon I rowed with Mr. Butler to another island in the broad waters of the Altamaha, called Tunno's Island, to return the visit of a certain Dr. Tunno, the proprietor of the island, named after him, as our rice swamp is after Major Butler. In the course of our visit a discussion arose as to the credibility of any negro assertion. No negro was to be believed on any occasion or any subject. No doubt they are habitual liars, for they are slaves; but there are some thrice honorable exceptions, who, being slaves, are yet not liars; and certainly the vice results much more from the circumstances in which they are placed than from any natural tendency to untruth in their case. The truth is that they are always considered as false and deceitful, and it is very seldom that any special investigation of the facts of any particular case is resorted to in their behalf. They are always prejudged on their supposed general characteristics, and never judged after the fact on the merit of any special instance.

On my return to our own island I visited another of the hospitals, and the settlements to which it belonged. The condition of these places and of their inhabitants is, of course, the same all over the plantation, and if I were to describe them I should but weary you with a repetition of identical phenomena: filthy, wretched, almost naked, always barelegged and barefooted children; negligent, ignorant, wretched mothers, whose apparent indifference to the plight of their offspring, and utter incapacity to alter it, are the inevitable result of their slavery. It is hopeless to attempt to reform their habits or improve their condition while the women are condemned to field labor; nor is it possible to overestimate the bad moral effect of the system as regards the women entailing this enforced separation from their children, and neglect of all the cares and duties of mother, nurse, and even housewife, which are all merged in the mere physical toil of a human hoeing machine.

It seems to me that the labor is not judiciously distributed in many cases—at least not as far as the women are concerned. It is true that every able-bodied woman is made the most of in being driven afield as long as, under all and any circumstances, she is able to wield a hoe; but, on the other hand, stout, hale, hearty girls and boys, of from eight to twelve and older, are allowed to lounge about, filthy and idle, with no pretense of an occupation but what they call "tend baby," *i.e.*, see to the life and limbs of the little slave infants, to whose mothers, working in distant fields, they carry them during the day to be suckled, and for the rest of the time leave them to crawl and kick in the filthy cabins or on the broiling sand which surrounds them, in which industry, excellent enough for the poor babies, these big lazy youths and lasses emulate them. Again, I find many women who have borne from five to ten children rated as workers, precisely as young women in the prime of their strength who have had none; this seems a cruel carelessness. To be sure, while the women are pregnant their task is diminished, and this is one of the many indirect inducements held out to reckless propagation, which has a sort of premium offered to it in the consideration of less work and more food, counterbalanced by none of the sacred responsibilities which hallow and ennoble the relation of parent and child; in short, as their lives are for the most part those of mere animals, their increase is literally mere animal breeding, to which every encouragement is given, for it adds to the master's live-stock and the value of his estate.

FLOGGING & THE SYSTEM

FEBRUARY 1839

TO-DAY I HAVE the pleasure of announcing to you a variety of improvements about to be made in the Infirmary of the island. There is to be a third story—a mere loft, indeed—added to the building; but, by affording more room for the least distressing cases of sickness to be drafted off into, it will leave the ground floor and room above it comparatively free for the most miserable of these unfortunates. To my unspeakable satisfaction, these destitute apartments are to be furnished with bedsteads, mattresses, pillows, and blankets; and I feel a little comforted for the many heartaches my life here inflicts upon me—at least some of my twinges will have wrought this poor alleviation of their wretchedness for the slaves when prostrated by disease or pain.

I had hardly time to return from the hospital home this morning before one of the most tremendous storms I ever saw burst over the island. On my return from the river I had a long and painful conversation with Mr. Butler upon the subject of the flogging which had been inflicted on the wretched Teresa. These discussions are terrible: they throw me into perfect agonies of distress for the slaves, whose position is utterly hopeless; for myself, whose intervention in their behalf sometimes seems to me worse than useless; for Mr. Butler, whose share in this horrible system fills me by turns with indignation and pity. But, after all, what can he do? How can he help it all? Moreover, born and bred in America, how should he care or wish to help it? And, of course, he does not; and I am in despair that he does not. He maintained that there had been neither hardship nor injustice in the case of Teresa's flogging; and that, moreover, she had not been flogged at all for complaining to me, but simply because her allotted task was not done at the appointed time. Of course this was the result of her having come to appeal to me instead of going to her labor; and as she knew perfectly well the penalty she was incurring, he maintained that there was neither hardship nor injustice in the case; the whole thing was a regularly established law, with which all the slaves were perfectly well acquainted; and this case was no exception whatever. The circumstance of my being on the island could not, of course, be allowed to overthrow the whole system of discipline established to secure the labor and obedience of the slaves; and if they chose to try experiments as to that fact, they and I must take the consequences. At the end of the day, the driver of the gang to which Teresa belongs reported her work not done, and Mr. O——— ordered him to give her the usual number of stripes, which order the driver of course obeyed, without knowing how Teresa had employed her time instead of hoeing. But Mr. O——— knew well enough, for the wretched woman told me that she had herself told him she should appeal to me about her weakness, and suffering, and inability to do the work exacted from her.

He did not, however, think proper to exceed in her punishment the usual number of stripes allotted to the nonperformance of the appointed daily task, and Mr. Butler pronounced the whole transaction perfectly satisfactory and *en règle*. The common drivers are limited in their powers of chastisement, not being allowed to administer more than a certain number of lashes to their fellow-slaves. Head man Frank, as he is called, has alone the privilege of exceeding this limit; and the overseer's latitude of infliction is only curtailed by the necessity of avoiding injury to life or limb. The master's irresponsible power has no such bound. When I was thus silenced on the particular case under discussion, I resorted, in my distress and indignation, to the abstract question, as I never can refrain from doing; and to Mr. Butler's assertion of the justice of poor Teresa's punishment, I retorted the manifest injustice of unpaid and enforced labor; the brutal inhumanity of allowing a man to strip and lash a woman, the mother of ten children; to exact from her toil which was to maintain in luxury two idle young men, the owners of the plantation. I said I thought female labor of the sort exacted from these slaves, and corporal chastisement such as they endure, must be abhorrent to any manly or humane man. Mr. Butler said he thought it was *disagreeable*, and left me to my reflections with that concession.

Mr. Butler has been anxious for a little while past that we should go down to St. Simon's, the cotton plantation. We shall suffer less from the heat, which I am beginning to find oppressive on this swamp island; and he himself wished to visit that part of his property, whither he had not yet been since our arrival in Georgia; so the day before yesterday he departed to make the necessary arrangements for our removal thither; and my time in the mean while has been taken up in fitting him out for his departure.

In the morning Jack and I took our usual paddle, and, having the tackle on board, tried fishing. I was absorbed in many sad and serious considerations until, after I know not how long a time elapsing without the shadow of a nibble, I was recalled to a most ludicrous perception of my ill success by Jack's sudden observation, "Missis, fishing berry good fun when um fish bite." This settled the fishing for that morning, and I let Jack paddle me down the broad turbid stream, endeavoring to answer in the most comprehensible manner to his keen but utterly undeveloped intellect the innumerable questions with which he plied me about Philadelphia, about England, about the Atlantic, etc. He dilated much upon the charms of St. Simon's, to which he appeared very glad that we were going; and, among other items of description, mentioned what I was very glad to hear, that it was a beautiful place for riding.

In the afternoon I saw Mr. Butler off for St. Simon's; it is fifteen miles lower down the river, and a large island at the very mouth of the Altamaha. The boat he went in was a large, broad, rather heavy, though well-built craft, by no means as swift or elegant as the narrow eight-oared long-boat in which he generally takes his walks on the water, but well adapted for the traffic between the two plantations, where it serves the purpose of a sort of omnibus or stage-coach for the transfer of the people from one to the other, and of a baggage-wagon or cart for the conveyance of all sorts of household goods, chattels, and necessaries. Mr. Butler sat in the middle of a perfect chaos of such freight; and as the boat pushed off, and the steersman took her into the stream, the men at the oars set up a chorus, which they continued to chant in unison with each other, and in time with their stroke, till the voices and oars were heard no more from the distance.

They all sing in unison, the tune and time they keep something quite wonderful. That which I have heard these people sing is often plaintive and pretty, but almost always has some resemblance to tunes with which they must have become acquainted through the instrumentality of white men, their overseers or masters whistling Scotch or Irish airs. The tune with which Mr. Butler's rowers started him down the Altamaha, as I stood at the steps to see him off, was a very distinct descendant of "Coming through the Rye." The words, however, were astonishingly primitive, especially the first line, which, when it burst from their eight throats in high unison, sent me into fits of laughter.

> *Jenny shake her toe at me,*
> *Jenny gone away*
> *Jenny shake her toe at me,*
> *Jenny gone away.*
> *Hurrah! Miss Susy, oh!*
> *Jenny gone away*
> *Hurrah! Miss Susy, oh!*
> *Jenny gone away.*

The pause made on the last "oh!" before the final announcement of her departure, had really a good deal of dramatic and musical effect. Except the extemporaneous chants in our honor, I have never heard the negroes on Mr. Butler's plantation sing any words that could be said to have any sense. To one, an extremely pretty, plaintive, and original air, there was but one line, which was repeated with a sort of wailing chorus—

Oh! my massa told me, there's no grass in Georgia.

Upon inquiring the meaning of which, I was told it was supposed to be the lamentation of a slave from one of the more northerly states, Virginia or Carolina, where the labor of hoeing the weeds, or grass as they call it, is not nearly so severe as here, in the rice and cotton lands of Georgia. Another very pretty and pathetic tune began with words that seemed to promise something sentimental—

Fare you well, and good-by, oh, oh!
I'm goin' away to leave you, oh, oh!

but immediately went off into nonsense verses about gentlemen in the parlor drinking wine and cordial, and ladies in the drawing-room drinking tea and coffee, etc.

In the evening, Mr. Butler's departure left me to the pleasures of an uninterrupted *tête-à-tête* with his cross-eyed overseer. I asked him several questions about some of the slaves who had managed to learn to read, and by what means they had been able to do so. As teaching them is strictly prohibited by the laws, they who instructed them, and such of them as acquired the knowledge, must have been not a little determined and persevering. This was my view of the case, of course, and of course it was not the overseer's. I asked him if many of Mr. Butler's slaves could read. He said "No; very few, he was happy to say, but those few were just so many too many." "Why, had he observed any insubordination in those who did?" And I reminded him of Cooper London, the Methodist preacher, whose performance of the burial service had struck me so much some time ago, to whose exemplary conduct and character there is but one concurrent testimony all over the plantation. No; he had no special complaint to bring against the lettered members of his subject community, but he spoke by anticipation. Every step they take toward intelligence and enlightenment lessens the probability of their acquiescing in their condition. Their condition is not to be changed—ergo, they had better not learn to read.

In all conversations that I have had with the Southerners upon these subjects, whether out of civility to what may be supposed to be an English-woman's prejudices, or a forlorn respect to their own convictions, the question of the fundamental wrong of slavery is generally admitted, or, at any rate, certainly never denied. That part of the subject is summarily dismissed, and all its other aspects vindicated, excused, and even lauded, with untiring eloquence. Of course, of the abstract question I could judge before I came here, but I confess I had not the remotest idea how absolutely my observation of every detail of the system, as a practical iniquity, would go to confirm my opinion of its abomination. Mr. O—— went on to condemn and utterly denounce all the preaching, and teaching, and moral instruction upon religious subjects which people in the South, pressed upon by Northern opinion, are endeavoring to give their slaves. Mr. O—— stated unequivocally his opinion that free labor would be more profitable on the plantations than the work of slaves, which, being compulsory, was of the worst possible quality and the smallest possible quantity; then the charge of them before and after they are able to work is onerous, the cost of feeding and clothing them very considerable, and, upon the whole, he, a Southern overseer, pronounced himself decidedly in favor of free labor, upon grounds of expediency. Having at the beginning of our conversation declined discussing the moral aspect of slavery, evidently not thinking that position tenable, I thought I had every right to consider Mr. Butler's slave-driver a decided Abolitionist.

I had been anxious to enlist his sympathies on behalf of my extreme desire to have some sort of garden, but did not succeed in inspiring him with my enthusiasm on the subject; he said there was but one garden that he knew of in the whole neighborhood of Darien, and that was our neighbor, old Mr. Couper's, a Scotchman on St. Simon's. I remembered the splendid gardenias on Tunno's Island, and referred to them as a proof of the material for ornamental gardening. He laughed, and said rice and cotton crops were the ornamental gardening principally admired by the planters, and that, to the best of his belief, there was not another decent kitchen or flower garden in the state but the one he had mentioned.

The next day after this conversation, I walked with my horticultural zeal much damped, and wandered along the dike by the broad river, looking at some pretty peach-trees in blossom, and thinking what a curse of utter stagnation this slavery produces, and how intolerable to me a life passed within its stifling influence would be. Think of peach-trees in blossom in the middle of February! It does seem cruel, with such a sun and soil, to be told that a garden is worth nobody's while here; however, Mr. O—— said that he believed the wife of the former overseer had made a "sort of a garden" at St. Simon's.

This morning, instead of my usual visit to the Infirmary, I went to look at the work and workers in the threshing mill: all was going on actively and orderly under the superintendence of head man Frank, with whom, and a very sagacious clever fellow who manages the steam power of the mill, and is honorably distinguished as Engineer Ned, I had a small chat. There is one among various drawbacks to the comfort and pleasure of our intercourse with these colored "men and brethren," at least in their slave condition, which certainly exercises my fortitude not a little—the swarms of fleas that cohabit with these sable dependents of ours are—well—incredible; moreover, they are by no means the only or most objectionable companions one borrows from them; and I never go to the Infirmary, where I not unfrequently am requested to look at very dirty limbs and bodies in very dirty draperies, without coming away with a strong inclination to throw myself into the water, and my clothes into the fire.

After leaving the mill I prolonged my walk, and came, for the first time, upon one of the "gangs," as they are called, in full field work. Upon my appearance and approach there was a momentary suspension of labor, and the usual chorus of screams and ejaculations of welcome, affection, and infinite desires for infinite small indulgences. I was afraid to stop their work, not feeling at all sure that urging a conversation with me would be accepted as any excuse for an uncompleted task, or avert the fatal infliction of the usual award of stripes; so I hurried off and left them to their hoeing.

On my way home I was encountered by London, our Methodist preacher, who accosted me with a request for a Prayer-book and Bible, and expressed his regret at hearing that we were so soon going to St. Simon's. I promised him his holy books, and asked him how he had learned to read, but found it impossible to get him to tell me. I wonder if he thought he should be putting his teacher, whoever he was, in danger of the penalty of the law against instructing the slaves, if he told me who he was.

After parting with him, I was assailed by a small gang of children, clamoring for the indulgence of some meat, which they besought me to give them. Animal food is only allowed to certain of the harder working men, hedgers and ditchers, and to them only occasionally, and in very moderate rations. My small cannibals clamored round me for flesh, as if I had had a butcher's cart in my pocket, till I began to laugh, and then to run, and away they came, like a pack of little black wolves, at my heels, shrieking, "Missis, you gib me piece meat—missis, you gib me meat," till I got home. At the door I found another petitioner, a young woman named Maria, who brought a fine child in her arms, and demanded a present of a piece of flannel. Upon my asking her who her husband was, she replied, without much hesitation, that she did not possess any such appendage. I gave another look at her bonny baby, and went into the house to get the flannel for her.

After I had been in the house a little while, I was summoned out again to receive the petition of certain poor women in the family-way to have their work lightened. I was, of course, obliged to tell them that I could not interfere in the matter; that their master was away, and that, when he came back, they must present their request to him: they said they had already begged "massa," and he had refused, and they thought, perhaps, if "missis" begged "massa" for them, he would lighten their task. Poor "missis," poor "massa," poor woman, that I am to have such prayers addressed to me! I had to tell them that, if they had already spoken to their master, I was afraid my doing so would be of no use, but that when he came back I would try; so, choking with crying, I turned away from them, and re-entered the house, to the chorus of "Oh, thank you, missis! God bless you, missis!"

In the evening I mentioned the petitions of these poor women to Mr. O——, thinking that perhaps he had the power to lessen their tasks. He seemed evidently annoyed at their having appealed to me; said that their work was not a bit too much for them, and that constantly they were *shamming* themselves in the family-way in order to obtain a diminution of their labor. Poor creatures! I suppose some of them do; but, again, it must be a hard matter for those who do not, not to obtain the mitigation of their toil which their condition requires.

JACK & MOLLY

FEBRUARY 1839

I THINK IT RIGHT to begin this letter with an account of a most prosperous fishing expedition Jack and I achieved the other morning. It is true we still occasionally drew up huge catfish, with their detestable beards and spikes, but we also captivated some magnificent perch, and the Altamaha perch are worth one's while both to catch and to eat. After leaving the boat on my return home, I encountered a curious creature walking all sideways, a small cross between a lobster and a crab. One of the negroes to whom I applied for its denomination informed me that it was a landcrab. I went a little farther and met with a snake; and, not being able to determine, at ignorant first sight, whether it was a malignant serpent or not, I ingloriously took to my heels, and came home on the full run. It is the first of these exceedingly displeasing animals I have encountered here; but Jack, for my consolation, tells me that they abound on St. Simon's, whither we are going—"rattlesnakes, and all kinds," says he, with an affluence of promise in his tone that is quite agreeable. Rattlesnakes will be quite enough of a treat, without the vague horrors that may be comprised in the additional "all kinds." Jack's account of the game on St. Simon's is really quite tantalizing to me. He says that partridges, woodcocks, snipe, and wild duck abound, so that, at any rate, our table ought to be well supplied. His account of the bears that are still to be found in the woods of the main land is not so pleasant, though he says they do no harm to the people if they are not meddled with.

As we were proceeding down the river, we met the flat, as it is called, a huge sort of clumsy boat, more like a raft than any other species of craft, coming up from St. Simon's with its usual swarthy freight of Mr. Butler's dependents from that place. I made Jack turn our canoe, because the universal outcries and exclamations very distinctly intimated that I should be expected to be at home to receive the homage of this cargo of "massa's people." No sooner, indeed, had I disembarked and reached the house, than a dark cloud of black life filled the piazza and swarmed up the steps, and I had to shake hands, like a popular president, till my arm ached at the shoulder-joint.

When this tribe had dispersed itself, a very old woman, with a remarkably intelligent, nice-looking young girl, came forward and claimed my attention. The old woman, who must, I think, by her appearance, have been near seventy, had been one of the house servants on St. Simon's Island in Major Butler's time, and retained a certain dignified courtesy and respectfulness of manner which is by no means an uncommon attribute of the better class of slaves. Old House Molly, after congratulating herself, with many thanks to heaven, for having spared her to see "massa's" wife and children, drew forward her young companion, and informed me she was one of her numerous grandchildren. Louisa made rather a shamefaced obeisance, and her old grandmother went on to inform me that she had only lately been forgiven by the overseer for an attempt to run away from the plantation. I inquired the cause of her desire to do so— a "thrashing" she had got for an unfinished task—"but lor, missis," explained the old woman, "taint no use— what use nigger run away?—de swamp all round; dey get in dar, an' dey starve to def, or de snakes eat 'em up—massa's nigger, dey don't neber run away."

After dismissing Molly and her granddaughter, I was about to re-enter the house, when I was stopped by Betty, head man Frank's wife, who came with a petition that she might be baptized. As usual with all requests involving any thing more than an immediate physical indulgence, I promised to refer the matter to Mr. Butler, but expressed some surprise that Betty, now by no means a young woman, should have postponed a ceremony which the religious among the slaves are apt to attach much importance to. She told me she had more than once applied for this permission to Massa King (the former overseer), but had never been able to obtain it, but that now she thought she would ask "de missis."

This woman was the wife of head man Frank, the most intelligent and trustworthy of Mr. Butler's slaves, the head driver. She was taken from him by the overseer left in charge of the plantation, the all-efficient and all-satisfactory Mr. King, and she had a son by him, whose straight features and diluted color, no less than his troublesome, discontented, and insubmissive disposition, bear witness to his Yankee descent. I do not know how long Mr. King's occupation of Frank's wife continued, or how the latter endured the wrong done to him. When

I visited the island Betty was again living with her husband—a grave, sad, thoughtful-looking man, whose admirable moral and mental qualities were extolled to me by no worse a judge of such matters than Mr. King himself.

BUTCHERING THE FOOD

FEBRUARY 1839

THE SPRING IS ALREADY HERE with her hands full
of flowers. I do not know who planted some straggling
pyrus japonica near the house, but it is blessing my eyes
with a hundred little flame-like buds, which will presently burst into a blaze; there are clumps of narcissus
roots sending up sheaves of ivory blossoms, and I actually
found a rose in bloom on the sunny side of one of the
dikes; what a delight they are in the slovenly desolation
of this abode of mine! What a garden one might have on
the banks of these dikes, with the least amount of trouble
and care!

In the afternoon I rowed over to Darien, and there
procuring the most miserable vehicle calling itself a carriage that I had ever seen. We drove some distance into
the sandy wilderness that surrounds the little town, to
pay a visit to some of the resident gentry who had called
upon us. The road was a deep, wearisome sandy track,
stretching wearisomely into the wearisome pine forest. From time to time a thicket of exquisite evergreen
shrubs broke the monotonous lines of the countless pine
shafts rising round us, and still more welcome were the

77

golden garlands of the exquisite wild jasmine, hanging, drooping, trailing, clinging, climbing through the dreary forest.

On our drive we passed occasionally a tattered man or woman, whose yellow mud complexion, straight features, and singularly sinister countenance bespoke an entirely different race from the negro population in the midst of which they lived. These are the so-called pine-landers of Georgia—filthy, lazy, ignorant, brutal, proud, penniless savages, without one of the nobler attributes which have been found occasionally allied to the vices of savage nature. They own no slaves, for they are almost without exception abjectly poor; they will not work, for that, as they conceive, would reduce them to an equality with the abhorred negroes; they squat, and steal, and starve, on the outskirts of this lowest of all civilized societies, and their countenances bear witness to the squalor of their condition and the utter degradation of their natures. To the crime of slavery, though they have no profitable part or lot in it, they are fiercely accessory, because it is the barrier that divides the black and white races, at the foot of which they lie wallowing in unspeakable degradation, but immensely proud of the base freedom which still separates them from the lash-driven tillers of the soil.

The house at which our call was paid was set down in the midst of the Pine Barren, with half-obliterated roads and paths round it, suggesting that it might be visited and was inhabited. It was large and not unhandsome, though curiously dilapidated, considering that people were actually living in it; certain remnants of carving on the cornices and paint on the panels bore witness to some former stage of existence less neglected and deteriorated than the present.

I must tell you something funny which occurred yesterday at dinner, which will give you some idea of the strange mode in which we live. The mutton we have here is some of the very best I have ever tasted, but it is invariably brought to table in lumps or chunks of no particular shape or size, and in which it is utterly impossible to recognize any part of the creature. Eat it, one may and does thankfully; name it, one could not by any possibility. Having submitted to this for some time, I at length inquired why a decent usual Christian joint of mutton—leg, shoulder, or saddle—was never brought to table: the reply was that the *carpenter* always cut up the meat, and that he did not know how to do it otherwise than by dividing it into so many thick square pieces, and proceeding to chop it up on that principle; and the consequence of this is, that four *lumps* or *chunks* are all that a whole sheep ever furnishes to our table by this artistic and economical process.

RICE MILL & TIDE MILL

FEBRUARY 1839

PASSING THE RICE MILL this morning in my walk, I went in to look at the machinery, the large steam mortars which shell the rice, and which work under the intelligent and reliable supervision of Engineer Ned. I was much surprised, in the course of conversation with him this morning, to find how much older a man he was than he appeared. Indeed, his youthful appearance had hitherto puzzled me much in accounting for his very superior intelligence and the important duties confided to him. He is, however, a man upward of forty years old, although he looks ten years younger. He attributed his own uncommonly youthful appearance to the fact of his never having done what he called field-work, or been exposed, as the common gang negroes are, to the hardships of their all but brutish existence. He said his former master had brought him up very kindly, and he had learned to tend the engines, and had never been put to any other work, but he said this was not the case with his poor wife. He wished she was as well off as he was, but she had to work in the rice-fields, and was "most broke in two" with labor, and exposure, and hard work while with child, and hard work just directly after child-bearing; he said she could hardly crawl, and he urged me very much to speak a kind word for her to massa. She was almost all the time in hospital, and he thought she could not live long.

On my return to the house I found a terrible disturbance in consequence of the disappearance from under Cook John's safe keeping of a ham Mr. Butler had committed to his charge. There was no doubt whatever that the unfortunate culinary slave had made away with the joint intended for our table: the very lies he told about it were so curiously shallow, child-like, and transparent, that while they confirmed the fact of his theft quite as much, if not more, than an absolute confession would have done, they provoked at once my pity and my irrepressible mirth to a most painful degree. Mr. Butler was in a state of towering anger and indignation, and, besides a flogging, sentenced the unhappy cook to degradation from his high and dignified position (and, alas! all its sweets of comparatively easy labor and good living from the remains of our table) to the hard toil, coarse scanty fare, and despised position of a common field-hand.

In speaking of this and the whole circumstance of John's trespass to Mr. Butler in the evening, I observed that the ignorance of these poor people ought to screen them from punishment. He replied that they knew well enough what was right and wrong. I asked how they could be expected to know it? He replied, by the means of Cooper London, and the religious instruction he gave them. So that, after all, the appeal is to be made against themselves to that moral and religious instruction which is withheld from them, and which, if they obtain it at all, is the result of their own unaided and unencouraged exertion. The more I hear, and see, and learn, and ponder the whole of this system of slavery, the more impossible I find it to conceive how its practisers and upholders are to justify their deeds before the tribunal of their own conscience or God's law. It is too dreadful to have those whom we love accomplices to this wickedness; it is too intolerable to find myself an involuntary accomplice to it.

I had a conversation the next morning with Abraham, Cook John's brother, upon the subject of his brother's theft. Abraham, a clever carpenter and much valued hand on the estate, went on, in answer to my questions, to tell me such a story that I declare to you I felt as if I could have howled with helpless indignation and grief when he departed and went to resume his work. His grandfather had been an old slave in Darien, extremely clever as a carpenter, and so highly valued for his skill and good character that his master allowed him to purchase his liberty by money which he earned by working for himself at odd times, when his task-work was over. I asked Abraham what sum his grandfather paid for his freedom: he said he did not know, but he supposed a large one, because of his being a "skilled carpenter," and so a peculiarly valuable chattel. Fourteen years after he became free, when he died, he had again amassed money to the amount of 700 dollars, which he left among his wife and children, the former being a slave on Major Butler's estate, where the latter remained by virtue of that fact slaves also. So this man not only bought his own freedom at a cost of *at least* 1000 dollars, but left a little fortune of 700 more at his death. This poor slave left, nevertheless, his children and grandchildren to the lot from which he had so heroically ransomed himself; and yet the white men with whom I live and talk tell me, day after day, that there is neither cruelty nor injustice in this accursed system.

About half past five I went to walk on the dikes, and met a gang of the field-hands going to the tide-mill, as the water served them for working then. Besides the great steam mill there is this, which is dependent on the rise and fall of the tide in the river, and where the people are therefore obliged to work by day or night, at whatever time the water serves to impel the wheel. They greeted me with their usual profusion of exclamations, petitions, and benedictions.

My letter has been interrupted by the breaking up of our residence on the rice plantation, and our arrival at St. Simon's, whence I now address you. We came down yesterday afternoon, and I was thankful enough of the fifteen miles' row to rest in, from the labor of leave-taking, with which the whole morning was taken up, and which, combined with packing and preparing all our own personalities and those of the children, was no sinecure. At every moment one or other of the poor people rushed in upon me to bid me good-by; many of their farewells were grotesque enough, some were pathetic, and all of them made me very sad. Poor people! How little I have done, how little I can do for them. I have worked my fingers nearly off with making, for the last day or two, innumerable rolls of coarse little baby-clothes, layettes for the use of small new-born slaves; Margery diligently cutting and shaping, and I as diligently stitching. We leave a good supply for the hospitals, and for the individual clients besides who have besieged me ever since my departure became imminent.

I had a long talk with that interesting and excellent man, Cooper London, who made an earnest petition that I would send him from the North a lot of Bibles and Prayer-books; certainly the science of reading must be much more common among the negroes than I supposed, or London must look to a marvelously increased spread of the same hereafter. There is, however, considerable reticence upon this point, or else the poor slaves must consider the mere possession of the holy books as good for salvation and as effectual for spiritual assistance to those who can not as to those who can comprehend them. Since the news of our departure has spread, I have had repeated eager entreaties for presents of Bibles and Prayer-books, and to my demurrer of "But you can't read, can you?" have generally received for answer a reluctant acknowledgment of ignorance, which, however, did not always convince me of the fact. In my farewell conversation with London I found it impossible to get him to tell me how he had learned to read: the penalties for teaching them are very severe—heavy fines, increasing in amount for the first and second offense, and imprisonment for the third. Such a man as London is certainly aware that to teach the slaves to read is an illegal act, and he may have been unwilling to betray whoever had been his preceptor even to my knowledge; at any rate, I got no answers from him but "Well, missis, me learn; well, missis, me try;" and finally, "Well, missis, me 'spose Heaven help me;" to which I could only reply that I knew Heaven was helpful, but very hardly to the tune of teaching folks their letters.

Our voyage from the rice to the cotton plantation was performed in the Lily, which looked like a soldier's baggage-wagon and an emigrant transport combined. Our crew consisted of eight men. Forward in the bow were miscellaneous live-stock, pots, pans, household furniture, kitchen utensils, and an indescribable variety of heterogeneous necessaries. Enthroned upon beds, bedding, tables, and other chattels, sat that poor pretty chattel Psyche, with her small chattel children. Midships sat the two tiny free women and myself, and in the stern Mr. Butler steering. We rowed down the huge stream, the men keeping time and tune to their oars with extemporaneous chants of adieu to the rice-island and those we left behind, and performed a spirited chant in honor of Psyche and our bouncing black housemaid, Mary.

At the end of a fifteen miles' row the conch was sounded, as at our arrival at the rice-island, and we made our descent on the famous long staple cotton island of St. Simon's, where we presently took up our abode in what had all the appearance of an old, half-decayed, rattling farm-house.

This morning, Sunday, I peeped round its immediate neighborhood, and saw, to my inexpressible delight, within hail, some noble-looking evergreen oaks, and close to the house itself a tiny would-be garden, a plot of ground with one or two peach-trees in full blossom, tufts of silver narcissus and jonquils, a quantity of violets and an exquisite myrtle bush; wherefore I said my prayers with especial gratitude.

FADED GRANDEUR

FEBRUARY 1839

THE PEOPLE that I saw yesterday were remarkably clean and tidy; to be sure, it was Sunday. The whole day, till quite late in the afternoon, the house was surrounded by a crowd of our poor dependents, waiting to catch a glimpse of Mr. Butler, myself, or the children; and until, from sheer weariness, I was obliged to shut the doors, an incessant stream poured in and out, whose various modes of salutation, greeting, and welcome were more grotesque and pathetic at the same time than any thing you can imagine.

In the afternoon I walked with Mr. Butler to see a new house in process of erection, which, when it is finished, is to be the overseer's abode and our residence during any future visits we may pay to the estate. I was horrified at the dismal site selected, and the hideous house erected on it. It is true that the central position is the principal consideration in the overseer's location; but both position and building seemed to me to witness to an inveterate love of ugliness, or, at any rate, a deadness to every desire of beauty, nothing short of horrible.

In every direction our view, as we returned, was

bounded by thickets of the most beautiful and various evergreen growth. Mr. Butler said, to my unutterable horror, that they were perfectly infested with rattlesnakes, and I must on no account go "beating about the bush" in these latitudes. We saw quantities of wild plum-trees all silvery with blossoms, and in lovely companionship and contrast with them a beautiful shrub covered with delicate pink bloom like flowering peach-trees. After that life in the rice-swamp, where the Altamaha kept looking over the dike at me all the time as I sat in the house writing or working, it is pleasant to be on *terra firma* again, and to know that the river is under my feet instead of over my head. The two plantations are of diametrically opposite dispositions—that is all swamp, and this all sand; or, to speak more accurately, that is all swamp, and all of this that is not swamp is sand.

I observed, among the numerous groups that we passed or met, a much larger proportion of mulattoes than at the rice-island; upon asking Mr. Butler why this was so, he said that there no white person could land without his or the overseer's permission, whereas on St. Simon's, which is a large island containing several plantations belonging to different owners, of course the number of whites, both residing on and visiting the place, was much greater, and the opportunity for intercourse between the blacks and whites much more frequent. While we were still on this subject, a horrid-looking filthy woman met us with a little child in her arms, a very light mulatto, whose extraordinary resemblance to Driver Bran (one of the officials who had been duly presented to me on my arrival, and who was himself a mulatto) struck me directly. I pointed it out to Mr. Butler, who merely answered, "Very likely his child." "And," said I, "did you never remark that Driver Bran is the exact image of Mr. King?" "Very likely his brother," was the reply: all which rather unpleasant state of relationships seemed accepted as such a complete matter of course, that I felt rather uncomfortable, and said no more about who was like who, but came to certain conclusions in my own mind as to a young lad who had been among our morning visitors, and whose extremely light color and straight, handsome features and striking resemblance to Mr. King had suggested suspicions of a rather unpleasant nature to me, and whose sole acknowledged parent was a very black negress of the name of Minda. I have no doubt at all, now, that he is another son of Mr. King, Mr. Butler's paragon overseer.

As we drew near the house again we were gradually joined by such a numerous escort of Mr. Butler's slaves that it was almost with difficulty we could walk along the path. They buzzed, and hummed, and swarmed round us like flies, and the heat and dust consequent upon this friendly companionship were a most unpleasant addition to the labor of walking in the sandy soil through which we were plowing. I was not sorry when we entered the house and left our body-guard outside.

I find here an immense proportion of old people; the work and the climate of the rice plantation require the strongest of the able-bodied men and women of the estate. The cotton crop is no longer by any means as paramount in value as it used to be, and the climate, soil, and labor of St. Simon's are better adapted to old, young, and feeble cultivators than the swamp fields of the rice-island. Such a decrease as this in the value of one's crop, and the steady increase at the same time of a slave population, now numbering between 700 and 800 bodies to clothe and house, mouths to feed, while the land is being exhausted by the careless and wasteful nature of the agriculture itself, suggests a pretty serious prospect of declining prosperity. The rice plantations are a great thing to fall back upon under these circumstances, and the rice crop is now quite as valuable, if not more so, than the cotton one on Mr. Butler's estates, once so famous and prosperous.

I find any number of all but superannuated men and women here, whose tales of the former grandeur of the estate and family are like things one reads of in novels. One old woman, who crawled to see me, and could hardly lift her poor bowed head high enough to look in my face, had been in Major Butler's establishment in Philadelphia, and told with infinite pride of having waited upon his daughters and granddaughters, Mr. Butler's sisters. Yet here she is, flung by like an old rag, crippled with age and disease, living, or rather dying by slow degrees in a miserable hovel, such as no decent household servant would at the North, I suppose, ever set their foot in. The poor old creature complained bitterly to me of all her ailments and all her wants. I had a visit from another tottering old crone called Dorcas, who all but went on her knees as she wrung and kissed my hands; with her came my friend Molly, the grandmother of the poor runaway girl Louisa, whose story I wrote you some little time ago. I had to hear it all over again, it being the newest event evidently in Molly's life; and it ended as before with the highly reasonable proposition: "Me say, missis, what for massa's niggar run away? Snake eat 'em up, or dey starve to def in a swamp. Massa's niggars dey don't neber run away."

89

HOUSE MOLLY

FEBRUARY 1839

I HAD A CURIOUS VISIT this morning from half a dozen of the women, among whom were Driver Morris's wife and Venus, Driver Bran's mother. They came especially to see the children, who are always eagerly asked for, and hugely admired. These poor women went into ecstasies over the little white pickaninnies, and were loud and profuse in their expressions of gratitude to Massa Butler for getting married and having children, a matter of thankfulness which, though it always makes me laugh very much, is a most serious one to them; for the continuance of the family keeps the estate and slaves from the hammer, and the poor wretches, besides seeing in every new child born to their owners a security against their own banishment from the only home they know, and separation from all ties of kindred and habit, and dispersion to distant plantations, not unnaturally look for a milder rule from masters who are the children of their father's masters. The relation of owner and slave may be expected to lose some of its harsher features, and, no doubt, in some instances, does so, when it is on each side the inheritance of successive generations. And so Mr.

Butler's slaves laud, and applaud, and thank, and bless him for having married, and endowed their children with two little future mistresses. One of these women, a Diana by name, went down on her knees, and uttered in a loud voice a sort of extemporaneous prayer of thanksgiving at our advent. Her "tanks to de good Lord God Almighty that missus had come, what give de poor niggar sugar and flannel," and "dat Massa Butler, him hab brought de missis and de two little misses down among de people," were really grotesque and yet certainly sincere.

I find the people here much more inclined to talk than those on the rice-island; they have less to do and more leisure, and bestow it very liberally on me. In a conversation with old "House Molly," as she is called, to distinguish her from all other Mollies on the estate, she having had the honor of being a servant in Major Butler's house for many years, I asked her if the relation between men and women who are what they call married, *i.e.*, who have agreed to live together as man and wife (the only species of marriage formerly allowed on the estate, I believe now London may read the Marriage Service to them), was considered binding by the people themselves and by the overseer. She said "not much formerly," and that the people couldn't be expected to have much regard to such an engagement, utterly ignored as it was by Mr. King, whose invariable rule, if he heard of any disagreement between a man and woman calling themselves married, was immediately to bestow them in "marriage" on other parties. Of course, the misery consequent upon such arbitrary destruction of voluntary and imposition of involuntary ties was nothing to Mr. King. I almost wish I was back again at the rice-island; for, though this is every way the pleasanter residence, I hear so much more that is intolerable of the treatment of the slaves from those I find here, that my life is really made wretched by it.

My letter was interrupted as usual by clamors for my presence at the door, and petitions for sugar, rice, and baby-clothes from a group of women who had done their tasks at three o'clock in the afternoon, and had come to say, "Ha do, missis?", and beg something on their way to their huts. Observing one among them whose hand was badly maimed, one finger being reduced to a mere stump, she told me it was in consequence of the bite of a rattlesnake, which had attacked and bitten her child, and then struck her as she endeavored to kill it; her little boy had died, but one of the drivers cut off her finger, and so she had escaped with the loss of that member only. It is yet too early in the season for me to make acquaintance with these delightful animals.

Tuesday, the 26th. I write to-day in great depression and distress. I have had a most painful conversation with Mr. Butler, who has declined receiving any of the people's petitions through me. Whether he is wearied with the number of these prayers and supplications, which he would escape but for me, as they probably would not venture to come so incessantly to him, and I, of course, feel bound to bring every one confided to me to him, or whether he has been annoyed at the number of pitiful and horrible stories of misery and oppression under the former rule of Mr. King, which have come to my knowledge since I have been here, and the grief and indignation caused, but which can not, by any means, always be done away with, though their expression may be silenced by his angry exclamations of "Why do you listen to such stuff?" or "Why do you believe such trash? Don't you know the niggers are all damned liars?" etc., I do not know; but he desired me this morning to bring him no more complaints or requests of any sort, as the people had hitherto had no such advocate, and had done very well without, and I was only kept in an incessant state of excitement with all the falsehoods they "found they could make me believe." It is indeed true that the sufferings of those who come to me for redress, and, still more, the injustice done to the great majority who can not, have filled my heart with bitterness and indignation that have overflowed my lips, till, I suppose, Mr. Butler is weary of hearing importunate pleading against wrongs that he will not even acknowledge, and for creatures whose common humanity with his own I half think he does not believe. This is no place for me, since I was not born among slaves, and can not bear to live among them.

Perhaps, after all, what he says is true: when I am gone they will fall back into the desperate uncomplaining habit of suffering, from which my coming among them, willing to hear and ready to help, has tempted them; he says that bringing their complaints to me, and the sight of my credulous commiseration, only tend to make them discontented and idle, and brings renewed chastisement upon them; and that so, instead of really befriending them, I am only preparing more suffering for them whenever I leave the place, and they can no more cry to me for help. And so I see nothing for it but to go and leave them to their fate; perhaps, too, he is afraid of the mere contagion of freedom which breathes from the very existence of those who are free; my way of speaking to the people, of treating them, of living with them, the appeals

93

I make to their sense of truth, of duty, of self-respect, the infinite compassion and the human consideration I feel for them.

Toward the afternoon yesterday I rowed up the river to the rice-island by way of refreshment to my spirits, and came back to-day, Wednesday, the 27th, through rather a severe storm. The wind was so high and the river so rough when I left the rice-island, that just as I was about to get into the boat I thought it might not be amiss to carry my life-preserver with me, and ran back to the house to fetch it. Having taken that much care for my life, I jumped into the boat, and we pushed off. The fifteen miles' row with a furious wind, and part of the time the tide against us, and the huge broad, turbid river broken into a foaming sea of angry waves, was a pretty severe task for the men. They pulled with a will, however, but I had to forego the usual accompaniment of their voices, for the labor was tremendous, especially toward the end of our voyage, where, of course, the nearness of the sea increased the roughness of the water terribly. The men were in great spirits, however (there were eight of them rowing, and one behind was steering); one of them said something which elicited an exclamation of general assent, and I asked what it was; the steerer said they were pleased because there was not another planter's lady in all Georgia who would have gone through the storm all alone with them in a boat; *i.e.*, without the protecting presence of a white man. "Why," said I, "my good fellows, if the boat capsized, or any thing happened, I am sure I should have nine chances for my life instead of one;" at this there was one shout of "So you would, missis; true for dat, missis;" and in great mutual good-humor we reached the landing at

Hampton Point. The idea of apprehending any mischief from them never yet crossed my brain; and in the perfect confidence with which I go among them, they must perceive a curious difference between me and my lady neighbors in these parts; all have expressed unbounded astonishment at my doing so.

The spring is fast coming on, and we shall, I suppose, soon leave Georgia. How new and sad a chapter of my life this winter here has been!

SLAVE VISITS

THIS MORNING I HAD a visit from two of the women, Charlotte and Judy, who came to me for help and advice for a complaint, which it really seems to me every other woman on the estate is cursed with, and which is a direct result of the conditions of their existence; the practice of sending women to labor in the fields in the third week after their confinement is a specific for causing this infirmity, and I know no specific for curing it under these circumstances. As soon as these poor things had departed with such comfort as I could give them, and the bandages they especially begged for, three other sable graces introduced themselves, Edie, Louisa, and Diana; the former told me she had had a family of seven children, but had lost them all through "ill luck," as she denominated the ignorance and ill treatment which were answerable for the loss of these, as of so many other poor little creatures their fellows.

Having dismissed her and Diana with the sugar and rice they came to beg, I detained Louisa, whom I had never seen but in the presence of her old grandmother, whose version of the poor child's escape to, and hiding in the woods, I had a desire to compare with the heroine's own story. She told it very simply, and it was most pathetic. She had not finished her task one day, when she said she felt ill, and unable to do so, and had been severely flogged by Driver Bran, in whose "gang" she then was. The next day, in spite of this encouragement to labor, she had again been unable to complete her appointed work; and Bran having told her that he'd tie her up and flog her if she did not get it done, she had left the field and run into the swamp. "Tie you up, Louisa!" said I; "what is that?" She then described to me that they were fastened up by their wrists to a beam or a branch of a tree, their feet barely touching the ground, so as to allow them no purchase for resistance or evasion of the lash, their clothes turned over their heads, and their backs scored with a leather thong, either by the driver himself, or, if he pleases to inflict their punishment by deputy, any of the men he may choose to summon to the office; it might be father, brother, husband, or lover, if the overseer so ordered it. "Oh," said I, "Louisa; but the rattlesnakes—the dreadful rattlesnakes in the swamps; were you not afraid of those horrible creatures?" "Oh, missis," said the poor child, "me no tink of dem; me forget all 'bout dem for de fretting." "Why did you come home at last?" "Oh, missis, me starve with hunger, me most dead with hunger before me come back." "And were you flogged, Louisa?" said I, with a shudder at what the answer might be. "No, missis, me go to hospital; me almost dead and sick so long, 'spec Driver Bran him forgot 'bout de flogging."

The wonderment of all my visitors at the exceedingly coarse and simple furniture and rustic means of comfort of my abode is very droll. I have never inhabited any apartment so perfectly devoid of what we should consider the common decencies of life; but to them, my rude chintz-covered sofa and common pine-wood table, with its green baize cloth, seem the adornings of a palace; and often in the evening, when I sit writing this daily history, the door of the great barn-like room is opened stealthily, and one after another, men and women come trooping silently in, their naked feet falling all but inaudibly on the bare boards as they betake themselves to the hearth, where they squat down on their hams in a circle, the bright blaze from the huge pine logs, which is the only light of this half of the room, shining on their sooty limbs and faces. I have had as many as fourteen at a time squatting silently there for nearly half an hour, watching me writing at the other end of the room. The candles on my table give only light enough for my own occupation, the fire-light illuminates the rest of the apartment; and you can not imagine any thing stranger than the effect of all these glassy whites of eyes and grinning white teeth turned toward me, and shining in the flickering light. I very often take no notice of them at all, and they seem perfectly absorbed in contemplating me. Sometimes at the end of my day's journal I look up and say suddenly, "Well, what do you want?" when each black figure springs up at once, as if moved by machinery; they all answer, "Me come say ha do (how d'ye do), missis;" and then they troop out as noiselessly as they entered, like a procession of sable dreams.

Two days ago I had a visit of great interest to me from several lads from twelve to sixteen years old, who had come to beg me to give them work. To make you understand this, you must know that, wishing very much to cut some walks and drives through the very picturesque patches of woodland not far from the house, I announced, through Jack, my desire to give employment in the wood-cutting line to as many lads as chose, when their unpaid task was done, to come and do some work for me, for which I engaged to pay them.

Friday, March 1. Last night, after writing so much, I felt weary, and went out into the air to refresh my spirit. The scene just beyond the house was beautiful; the moon-light slept on the broad river, which here is almost the sea, and on the masses of foliage of the great Southern oaks; the golden stars shone in the purple curtains of the night, and the measured rush of the Atlantic unfurling its huge skirts upon the white sands of the beach (the sweetest and most awful lullaby in nature) resounded through the silent air.

All the slaves' huts on St. Simon's are far less solid, comfortable, and habitable than those at the rice-island. I do not know whether the laborer's habitation bespeaks the alteration in the present relative importance of the crops, but certainly the cultivators of the once far-famed long staple sea-island cotton of St. Simon's are far more miserably housed than the rice-raisers of the other plantation. These ruinous shielings, that hardly keep out wind or weather, are deplorable homes for young or aged people, and poor shelters for the hard-working men and women who cultivate the fields in which they stand.

As I was cantering along the side of one of the cotton-fields I suddenly heard some inarticulate vehement cries, and saw what seemed to be a heap of black limbs tumbling and leaping toward me, renewing the screams at intervals as it approached. I stopped my horse, and the black ball bounded almost into the road before me, and, suddenly straightening itself up into a haggard hag of a half-naked negress, exclaimed, with panting, eager breathlessness, "Oh, missis, missis, you no hear me cry, you no hear me call. Oh, missis, me call, me cry, and me run; make me a gown like dat. Do, for massy's sake, only make me a gown like dat." This modest request for a riding habit in which to hoe the cotton-fields served for an introduction to sundry other petitions for rice, and sugar, and flannel, all which I promised the petitioner, but not the "gown like dat;" whereupon I rode off, and she flung herself down in the middle of the road to get her wind and rest.

Yesterday evening I had a visit that made me very sorrowful, if any thing connected with these poor people can be called more especially sorrowful than their whole condition; but Mr. Butler's declaration that he will receive no more statements of grievances or petitions for redress through me makes me as desirous now of shunning the vain appeals of these unfortunates as I used to be of receiving and listening to them. The imploring cry, "Oh missis!" that greets me whichever way I turn, makes me long to stop my ears now; for what can I say or do any more for them? The poor little favors—the rice, the sugar, the flannel—that they beg for with such eagerness, and receive with such exuberant gratitude, I can, it is true, supply, and words and looks of pity, and counsel of patience, and such instruction in womanly habits of decency and cleanliness as may enable them to better, in some degree, their own hard lot; but to the entreaty, "Oh, missis, you speak to massa for us! Oh, missis, you beg massa for us! Oh, missis, you tell massa for we, he sure do as you say!" I can not now answer as formerly, and I turn away choking and with eyes full of tears from the poor creatures, not even daring to promise any more the faithful transmission of their prayers.

The women who visited me yesterday evening were all in the family-way, and came to entreat of me to have the sentence (what else can I call it?) modified which condemns them to resume their labor of hoeing in the fields three weeks after their confinement. They knew, of course, that I can not interfere with their appointed labor, and therefore their sole entreaty was that I would use my influence with Mr. Butler to obtain for them a month's respite from labor in the field after childbearing. Their principal spokeswoman, a woman with a bright sweet face, called Mary, and a very sweet voice, implored me to have a kind of labor given to them less exhausting during the month after their confinement. I held the table before me so hard in order not to cry that I think my fingers ought to have left a mark on it. I told them that Mr. Butler had forbidden me to bring him any more complaints from them, for that he thought the ease with which I received and believed their stories only tended to make them discontented, and that, therefore, I feared I could not promise to take their petitions to him; but that he would be coming down to "the Point" soon, and that they had better come then some time when I was with him, and say what they had just been saying to me; and with this, and various small bounties, I was forced, with a heavy heart, to dismiss them; and when they were gone, with many exclamations of, "Oh yes, missis, you will, you will speak to massa for we; God bless you, missis, we sure you will!" I had to cry out for them, for myself, for *us*. How I do ponder upon the strange fate which has brought me here.

St. Annie's is the remotest settlement on the whole

plantation, and I found there the wretchedest huts, and most miserably squalid, filthy, and forlorn creatures I had yet seen here—certainly the condition of the slaves on this estate is infinitely more neglected and deplorable than that on the rice plantation. Perhaps it has something to do with the fact that the climate on St. Simon's is generally considered peculiarly mild and favorable, and so less protection of clothes and shelter is thought necessary here for the poor residents; perhaps, too, it may be because the plantation here, which was once the chief source of its owner's wealth, is becoming a secondary one, and so not worth so much care or expense in repairing and constructing negro huts and feeding and clothing the slaves. More pitiable objects than some of those I saw at the St. Annie's settlement to-day I hope never to see: there was an old crone called Hannah, a sister, as well as I could understand what she said, of old House Molly, whose face and figure, seamed with wrinkles, and bowed and twisted with age and infirmity, really hardly retained the semblance of those of a human creature, and as she crawled to me almost half her naked body was exposed through the miserable tatters that she held on with one hand, while the other eagerly clutched my hand, and her poor blear eyes wandered all over me as if she was bewildered by the strange aspect of any human being but those whose sight was familiar to her. One or two forlorn creatures like herself, too old or too infirm to be compelled to work, and the half-starved and more than half-naked children apparently left here under their charge, were the only inmates I found in these wretched hovels.

After reaching home I went to the house of the overseer to see his wife, a tidy, decent, kind-hearted little woman, who seems to me to do her duty by the poor people she lives among as well as her limited intelligence and still more limited freedom allow. The house her husband lives in is the former residence of Major Butler, which was the great mansion of the estate. It is now in a most ruinous and tottering condition, and they inhabit but a few rooms in it; the others are gradually mouldering to pieces. Old Molly, of whom I have often before spoken to you, who lived here in the days of the prosperity and grandeur of Hampton, still clings to the relics of her old master's former magnificence, and with pride showed me through the dismantled decaying rooms and over the remains of the dairy, displaying a capacious fish-box or well, where, in the good old days, the master's supply was kept in fresh salt water till required for table. I could not help contrasting the present state of the estate with that which she described, and wondering why it should have become, as it undoubtedly must have done, so infinitely less productive a property than in the old Major's time.

Before closing, I have a mind to transcribe the entries for to-day recorded in a sort of day-book, where I put down very succinctly the number of people who visit me, their petitions and ailments, and also such special particulars concerning them as seem to me worth recording. You will see how miserable the physical condition of many of these poor creatures is. The people on this plantation are well off, and consider themselves well off, in comparison with the slaves on some of the neighboring estates.

Fanny has had six children; all dead but one. She came to beg to have her work in the field lightened.

Nanny has had three children; two of them are dead.

She came to implore that the rule of sending them into the field three weeks after their confinement might be altered.

Leah, Caesar's wife, has had six children; three are dead.

Sophy, Lewis's wife, came to beg for some old linen. She is suffering fearfully; has had ten children; five of them are dead. The principal favor she asked was a piece of meat, which I gave her.

Sally, Scipio's wife, has had two miscarriages and three children born, one of whom is dead. She came complaining of incessant pain and weakness in her back. This woman was a mulatto daughter of a slave called Sophy, by a white man of the name of Walker, who visited the plantation.

Charlotte, Renty's wife, had had two miscarriages, and was with child again. She was almost crippled with rheumatism, and showed me a pair of poor swollen knees that made my heart ache. I have promised her a pair of flannel trowsers, which I must forthwith set about making.

Sarah, Stephen's wife—this woman's case and history were alike deplorable. She had had four miscarriages, had brought seven children into the world, five of whom were dead, and was again with child. She complained of dreadful pains in the back, and an internal tumor which swells with the exertion of working in the fields; probably, I think, she is ruptured. She told me she had once been mad and had ran into the woods, where she contrived to elude discovery for some time, but was at last tracked and brought back, when she was tied up by the arms, and heavy logs fastened to her feet, and was severely flogged. After this she contrived to escape again, and lived for some time skulking in the woods, and she supposes mad, for when she was taken again she was entirely naked. She subsequently recovered from this derangement, and seems now just like all the other poor creatures who come to me for help and pity. I suppose her constant childbearing and hard labor in the fields at the same time may have produced the temporary insanity.

Sukey, Bush's wife, only came to pay her respects. She had had four miscarriages; had brought eleven children into the world, five of whom are dead.

Molly, Quambo's wife, also only came to see me. Hers was the best account I have yet received; she had had nine children, and six of them were still alive.

DE BEAUTIFULLEST SHEEP

MARCH 1839

I HAVE OFTEN WRITTEN that we have mutton here but such is the barbarous ignorance of the cook, or rather the butcher who furnishes our kitchen supplies, that I defy the most expert anatomist to pronounce on any piece (joints they can not be called) of mutton brought to our table to what part of the animal sheep it originally belonged. I have often complained bitterly of this, and in vain implored Abraham, the cook, to send me some dish of mutton to which I might with safety apply the familiar name of leg, shoulder, or haunch. These remonstrances and expostulations have produced no result whatever, however, but an increase of eccentricity in the *chunks* of sheeps' flesh placed upon the table; the squares, diamonds, cubes, and rhomboids of mutton have been more ludicrous and hopeless with every fresh endeavor Abraham has made to find out "zackly wot de missis do want."

So the day before yesterday, Abraham appeared at the door of the room brandishing a very long thin knife, and with many bows, grins, and apologies for disturbing me, begged that I would go and cut up a sheep for him.

My first impulse, of course, was to decline the very unusual task offered me with mingled horror and amusement. Abraham, however, insisted and besought, extolled the fineness of his sheep, declared his misery at being unable to cut it as I wished, and his readiness to conform for the future to whatever *patterns* of mutton "de missis would only please to give him." Upon reflection, I thought I might very well contrive to indicate upon the sheep the size and form of the different joints of civilized mutton, and so, for the future, save much waste of good meat. And so I followed Abraham to the kitchen, when, with a towel closely pinned over my silk dress, and knife in hand, I stood for a minute or two meditating profoundly before the rather unsightly object which Abraham had pronounced "de beautifullest sheep de missis eber saw." I screwed my courage to the sticking-point, and slowly and delicately traced out with the point of my long carving-knife two shoulders, two legs, a saddle, and a neck of mutton. As an accompaniment to "de beautifullest mutton de missis eber see," we have just received from my neighbor Mr. Couper the most magnificent supply of fresh vegetables, green peas, salad, etc. He has a garden, and a Scotchman's real love for horticulture, and I profit by them in this very agreeable manner.

I have been interrupted by several visits, among others, one from a poor creature called Judy, whose sad story and condition affected me most painfully. She had been married, she said, some years ago to one of the men called Temba, who, however, now has another wife, having left her because she went mad. While out of her mind she escaped into the jungle, and contrived to secrete herself there for some time, but was finally tracked and caught, and brought back and punished by being made to sit, day after day, for hours in the stocks—a severe punishment for a man, but for a woman perfectly barbarous. She complained of chronic rheumatism, and other terrible ailments, and said she suffered such intolerable pain while laboring in the fields, that she had come to entreat me to have her work lightened. She could hardly crawl, and cried bitterly all the time she spoke to me.

She told me a miserable story of her former experience on the plantation under Mr. King's overseership. It seems that Jem Valiant, a mulatto lad, was her first-born, the son of Mr. King, who forced her, flogged her severely for having resisted him, and then sent her off, as a farther punishment, to Five Pound—a horrible swamp in a remote corner of the estate, to which the slaves are sometimes banished. This poor creature said that, bad as the flogging was, she would sooner have taken that again than the dreadful lonely days and nights she spent on the penal swamp of Five Pound.

DISMAL STORIES

MARCH 1839

I HAVE HAD an uninterrupted stream of women and children flowing in the whole morning to say "Ha de, missis?" Among others, a poor woman called Mile, who could hardly stand for pain and swelling in her limbs; she had had fifteen children and two miscarriages; nine of her children had died; for the last three years she had become almost a cripple with chronic rheumatism, yet she is driven every day to work in the field. She held my hands, and stroked them in the most appealing way while she exclaimed, "Oh my missis! My missis! Me neber sleep till day for de pain," and with the day her labor must again be resumed. I gave her flannel and sal volatile to rub her poor swelled limbs with; rest I could not give her—rest from her labor and her pain—this mother of fifteen children.

Another of my visitors had a still more dismal story to tell; her name was Die; she had had sixteen children, fourteen of whom were dead; she had had four miscarriages: one had been caused with falling down with a very heavy burden on her head, and one from having her arms strained up to be lashed. I asked her what she meant by having her arms tied up. She said their hands were first tied together, sometimes by the wrists, and sometimes, which was worse, by the thumbs, and they were then drawn up to a tree or post, so as almost to swing them off the ground, and then their clothes rolled round their waist, and a man with a cowhide stands and stripes them. I give you the woman's words. She did not speak of this as of any thing strange, unusual, or especially horrid and abominable; and when I said, "Did they do that to you when you were with child?" she simply replied, "Yes, missis." And to all this I listen—I, an English woman, the wife of the man who owns these wretches, and I can not say, "That thing shall not be done again; that cruel shame and villainy shall never be known here again." I gave the woman meat and flannel, which were what she came to ask for, and remained choking with indignation and grief long after they had all left me to my most bitter thoughts. I went out to try and walk off some of the weight of horror and depression which I am beginning to feel daily more and more, surrounded by all this misery and degradation that I can neither help nor hinder.

MY NEW APARTMENT

MARCH 1839

I HAVE HAD, as usual, a tribe of visitors and petitioners. I will give you an account of those cases which had any thing beyond the average of interest in their details. One poor woman, named Molly, came to beg that I would, if possible, get an extension of their exemption from work after childbearing. The close of her argument was concise and forcible. "Missis, we hab um pickanniny— tree weeks in de ospital, and den right out upon the hoe again—*can we strong* dat way, missis? No!" And truly I do not see that they can. This poor creature has had eight children and two miscarriages. All her children were dead but one. Another of my visitors was named Venus; it is a favorite name among these sable folk. I could not understand how she came on this property, for she was the daughter of a black woman and the overseer of an estate to which her mother formerly belonged, and from which I suppose she was sold, exchanged, or given, as the case may be, to the owners of this plantation. She was terribly crippled with rheumatism, and came to beg for some flannel. She had had eleven children, five of whom had died, and two miscarriages. As she took her departure, the vacant space she left on the other side of my writing-table was immediately filled by another black figure with a bowed back and piteous face, one of the thousand "Mollies" on the estate, where the bewildering redundancy of their name is avoided by adding that of their husband; so when the question, "Well, who are you?" was answered with the usual genuflexion, and "I'se Molly, missis!" I, of course, went on with "whose Molly," and she went on to refer herself to the ownership (under Mr. Butler and heaven) of one Tony, but proceeded to say that he was not her *real* husband. This appeal to an element of reality in the universally accepted fiction which passes here by the title of marriage surprised me; and on asking her what she meant, she replied that her real husband had been sold from the estate for repeated attempts to run away. He had made his escape several times, and skulked starving in the woods and morasses, but had always been tracked and brought back, and flogged almost to death, and finally sold as an incorrigible runaway. I do not write you the poor woman's jargon, which was ludicrous; for I can not write you the sighs, and tears, and piteous looks, and gestures, that made it pathetic; of course she did not know whither or to whom her *real* husband had been sold; but in the mean time Mr. King, that merciful Providence of the estate, had provided her with the above-named Tony, by whom she had had nine children, six of whom were dead; she, too, had miscarried twice. She came to ask me for some flannel for her legs, which were all swollen with constant rheumatism, and to beg me to give her something to cure some bad sores and ulcers, which seemed to me dreadful enough in their present condition, but which she said break out afresh and are twice as bad every summer.

I rode with Hector, who has a good deal to do with the horses, and so had volunteered to accompany me, being one of the few negroes on the estate who can sit on a horse. In the course of our conversation, Hector divulged certain opinions relative to the comparative gentility of driving in a carriage and the vulgarity of walking, which sent me into fits of laughing; at which he grinned sympathetically, and opened his eyes very wide, but certainly without attaining the least insight into what must have appeared to him my very unaccountable and unreasonable merriment. Among various details of the condition of the people on the several estates on the island, he told me that a great number of the men on all the different plantations had *wives* on the neighboring estates as well as on that to which they properly belonged. "Oh, but," said I, "Hector, you know that can not be; a man has but one lawful wife." Hector knew this, he said, and yet seemed puzzled himself, and rather puzzled me to account for the fact, that this extensive practice of bigamy was perfectly well known to the masters and overseers, and never in any way found fault with or interfered with.

My whole afternoon was spent in shifting my bed and bedroom furniture from a room on the ground floor to one above. My new apartment is what I should call decidedly airy; the window, unless when styled by courtesy shut, which means admitting of draught enough to blow a candle out, must be wide open, being incapable of any intermediate condition; the latch of the door, to speak the literal truth, does shut; but it is the only part of it that does—that is, the latch and the hinges; every where else its configuration is traced by a distinct line of light and air. I now discover to my dismay, having transported every other article of bedroom furniture to this new room, it is impossible to introduce the wardrobe for my clothes. Well, our stay here is drawing to a close, and therefore these small items of discomfort can not afflict me much longer.

Among my visitors to-day was a poor woman named Oney, who told me her husband had gone away from her now for four years; it seems he was the property of Mr. King, and when that gentleman went to slave-driving on his own account, and ceased to be the overseer of this estate, he carried her better half, who was his chattel, away with him, and she never expects to see him again. After her departure I had a most curious visitor, a young mulatto lad of the name of Renty. He was evidently, in his own opinion, a very superior creature, and yet, as his conversation with me testified, he was conscious of some flaw in the honor of his "yellow" complexion. "Who is your mother, Renty?" said I. "Betty, head man Frank's wife." I was rather dismayed at the promptness of this reply, and hesitated a little at my next question, "Who is your father?" My sprightly young friend, however, answered, without an instant's pause, "Mr. King." Here I came to a halt, and, willing to suggest some doubt to the lad, because for many peculiar reasons this statement seemed to me shocking, I said, "What, old Mr. King?" "No, Massa Roswell." "Did your mother tell you so?" "No, missis, me ashamed to ask her; Mr. Couper's children told me so, and I 'spect they know it."

Tuesday, March 3. This morning, old House Molly, coming from Mr. Gowen's upon some errand to me, I asked her if Renty's statement was true; she confirmed the whole story, and, moreover, added that this connection took place after Betty was married to head man

Frank. He is the chief man at the rice-island, second in authority to Mr. O——, and, indeed, for a considerable part of the year, absolute master and guardian during the night of all the people and property at the rice plantation; for, after the early spring, the white overseer himself is obliged to betake himself to the main land to sleep, out of the influence of the deadly malaria of the rice swamp, and Frank remains sole sovereign of the island from sunset to sunrise—in short, during the whole period of his absence. Mr. Butler bestowed the highest commendations upon his fidelity and intelligence, and, during the visit Mr. Roswell King paid us at the island, he was emphatic in his praise of both Frank and his wife. Frank is a serious, sad, sober-looking, very intelligent man; I should think he would not relish having his wife borrowed from him.

I must give you an idea of the sort of service one is liable to obtain from one's most intelligent and *civilized* servants hereabouts, and the consequent comfort and luxury of one's daily existence. Yesterday Aleck, the youth who fulfills the duties of what you call a waiter, and we in England a footman, gave me a salad for dinner, mixed with so large a portion of the soil in which it had grown that I requested him to-day to be kind enough to wash the lettuce before he brought it to table. Margery later in the day told me that he had applied to her very urgently for soap and a brush, "as missis wished de lettuce *scrubbed.*"

HOUSE MOLLY'S CABIN

MARCH 1839

I HAVE BEEN LONG PROMISING poor old House
Molly to visit her in her own cabin, and so the day before yesterday I walked round the settlement to her
dwelling, and a most wretched hovel I found it. She has
often told me of the special directions left by her old master for the comfort and well-being of her old age, and
certainly his charge has been but little heeded by his heirs,
for the poor faithful old slave is most miserably off in
her infirm years. She made no complaint, however, but
seemed overjoyed at my coming to see her. She took
me to the hut of her brother, old Jacob, where the same
wretched absence of every decency and every comfort
prevailed; but neither of them seemed to think the condition that appeared so wretched to me one of peculiar
hardship—though Molly's former residence in her master's house might reasonably have made her discontented
with the lot of absolute privation to which she was now
turned over—but, for the moment, my visit seemed to
compensate for all sublunary sorrows, and she and poor
old Jacob kept up a duet of rejoicing at my advent, and
that I had brought "de little missis among um people

afore they die." Leaving them, I went on to the house of Jacob's daughter Hannah, with whom Psyche, the wife of his son Joe, lives. I found their cabin as tidy and comfortable as it could be made, and their children, as usual, neat and clean; they are capital women, both of them, with an innate love of cleanliness and order most uncommon among these people.

On my way home I overtook two of my daily suppliants, who were going to the house in search of me, and meat, flannel, rice, and sugar, as the case might be; they were both old and infirm-looking women, and one of them, called Scylla, was extremely lame, which she accounted for by an accident she had met with while carrying a heavy weight of rice on her head; she had fallen on a sharp stake, or snag, she called it, and had never recovered from the injury she had received. She complained also of falling of the womb. Her companion was a cheery soul who complained of nothing, but begged for flannel. I asked her about her family and children; she had no children left, nothing but grandchildren; she had had nine children, and seven of them died quite young; the only two who grew up left her to join the British when they invaded Georgia in the last war, and their children, whom they left behind, were all her family now.

In the afternoon I made my first visit to the hospital of the estate, and found it, as indeed I find every thing else here, in a far worse state even than the wretched establishments on the rice-island, dignified by that name. The floor (which was not boarded, but merely the damp hard earth itself) was strewn with wretched women, who, but for their moans of pain, and uneasy, restless motions, might very well each have been taken for a mere heap of filthy rags; the chimney refusing passage to the smoke from the pine-wood fire, it puffed out in clouds through the room, where it circled and hung, only gradually oozing away through the windows, not a single whole pane of glass in them. My eyes, unaccustomed to the turbid atmosphere, smarted and watered, and refused to distinguish at first the different dismal forms, from which cries and wails assailed me in every corner of the place.

Having given kind words and promises of help, I went on to what seemed a yet more wretched abode. This was a room where there was no fire because there was no chimney, and where the holes made for windows had no panes or glasses in them. The place was so dark that, on first entering it, I was afraid to stir lest I should fall over some of the deplorable creatures extended upon the floor. As soon as they perceived me, one cry of "Oh missis!" rang through the darkness; and it really seemed to me as if I was never to exhaust the pity, and amazement, and disgust which this receptacle of suffering humanity was to excite in me. The poor dingy supplicating sleepers upraised themselves as I cautiously advanced among them; those who could not rear their bodies from the earth held up piteous beseeching hands, and as I passed from one to the other I felt more than one imploring clasp laid upon my dress. One poor woman, called Tressa, who was unable to speak above a whisper from utter weakness and exhaustion, told me she had had nine children, was suffering from incessant flooding, and felt "as if her back would split open." There she lay, a mass of filthy tatters, without so much as a blanket under her or over her, on the bare earth in this chilly darkness. I promised them help and comfort, beds and blankets, and light and fire—that is, I promised to ask Mr. Butler for all this for them; and, in the very act of doing so, I remembered with a sudden pang of anguish that I was to urge no more petitions for his slaves to their master.

I groped my way out, and, emerging on the piazza, all the choking tears and sobs I had controlled broke forth, and I leaned there crying over the lot of these unfortunates till I heard a feeble voice of "Missis, you no cry; missis, what for you cry?" and, looking up, saw a poor crippled old man, lying in the corner of the piazza, unable even to crawl toward me. By his side sat a young woman, the expression of whose face was the most suffering, and, at the same time, the most horribly repulsive I ever saw. I found she was, as I supposed, half-witted; and, on coming nearer to inquire into her ailments and what I could do for her, found her suffering from that horrible disease—I believe some form of scrofula—which attacks and eats away the joints of the hands and fingers —a more hideous and loathsome object I never beheld; her name was Patty, and she was granddaughter to the old crippled creature by whose side she was squatting.

I wandered home, stumbling with crying as I went, and feeling so utterly miserable that I really hardly saw where I was going, for I as nearly as possible fell over a great heap of oyster-shells left in the middle of the path. This is a horrid nuisance, which results from an indulgence which the people here have and value highly; the waters round the island are prolific in shell-fish, oysters, and the most magnificent prawns I ever saw. The former are a considerable article of the people's diet, and the shells are allowed to accumulate, as they are used in the composition of which their huts are built, and which is a sort of combination of mud and broken oyster-shells, which forms an agglomeration of a kind very solid and durable for such building purposes; but, instead of being all carried to some specified place out of the way, these great heaps of oyster-shells are allowed to be piled up any where and every where, forming the most unsightly obstructions in every direction. As masters have been scarce on this plantation for many years now, a mere unsightliness is not a matter likely to trouble any body much.

CHURCH

MARCH 1839

THIS LETTER HAS REMAINED unfinished, and my journal interrupted for more than a week. Mr. Butler has been quite unwell, and I have been traveling to and fro daily between Hampton and the rice-island in the long-boat to visit him; for the last three days I have remained at the latter place, and only returned here this morning early. My daily voyages up and down the river have introduced me to a great variety of new musical performances of our boatmen, who invariably, when the rowing is not too hard, moving up or down with the tide, accompany the stroke of their oars with the sound of their voices. I told you formerly that I thought I could trace distinctly some popular national melody with which I was familiar in almost all their songs; but I have been quite at a loss to discover any such foundation for many that I have heard lately, and which have appeared to me extraordinarily wild and unaccountable. The way in which the chorus strikes in with the burden, between each phrase of the melody chanted by a single voice, is very curious and effective, especially with the rhythm of the rowlocks for accompaniment. The high voices all in unison, and the admirable time and true accent with which their responses are made, always make me wish that some great musical composer could hear these semi-savage performances.

I have now settled down at Hampton again; Mr. Butler is quite recovered, and is coming down here in a day or two for change of air; it is getting too late for him to stay on the rice plantation even in the day, I think. You can not imagine any thing so exquisite as the perfect curtains of yellow jasmine with which this whole island is draped; and as the boat comes sweeping down toward the Point, the fragrance from the thickets hung with their golden garlands greets one before one can distinguish them; it is really enchanting.

I have now to tell you my hallowing last Sunday by gathering a congregation of the people into my big sitting-room, and reading prayers to them. I had been wishing very much to do this for some time past, and obtained Mr. Butler's leave while I was with him at the rice-island. Some of the people are allowed to go up to Darien once a month to church; but, with that exception, they have no religious service on Sunday whatever for them. There is a church on the island of St. Simon, but they are forbidden to frequent it, as it leads them off their own through neighboring plantations, and gives opportunities for meetings between the negroes of the different estates, and very likely was made the occasion of abuses and objectionable practices of various kinds; at any rate, Mr. King forbade the Hampton slaves resorting to the St. Simon's church, and so for three Sundays in the month they are utterly without Christian worship or teaching, or any religious observance of God's day whatever.

I told the house servants that if they would come to

the sitting-room at eleven o'clock, I would read prayers to them, and that they might tell any of their friends or any of the people that I should be very glad to see them if they liked to come. Accordingly, most of those who live at the Point, *i.e.*, in the immediate neighborhood of the house, came, and it was encouraging to see the very decided efforts at cleanliness and decorum of attire which they had all made. There was something in my relation to the poor people by whom I was surrounded that touched me so deeply that I found it difficult to command my voice, and had to stop several times in order to do so. When I had done, they all with one accord uttered the simple words, "We thank you, missis," and instead of overwhelming me as usual with petitions and complaints, they rose silently and quietly.

MR. COUPER & SOPHY

MARCH 1839

M y   v i s i t   to my neighbor Mr. Couper pleased and interested me very much. He is an old Glasgow man, who has been settled here many years. It is curious how many of the people round this neighborhood have Scotch names; it seems strange to find them thus gathered in the vicinity of a new Darien. Mr. Couper's house is a roomy, comfortable, handsomely laid-out mansion, to which he received me with very cordial kindness, and where I spent part of a very pleasant morning, talking with him, hearing all he could tell me of the former history of Mr. Butler's plantation. His description of its former master, old Major Butler, and of his agent and overseer Mr. King, and of that gentleman's son and successor the late overseer, interested me very much; of the two latter functionaries his account was terrible, and much what I had supposed any impartial account of them would be; because, let the propensity to lying of the poor wretched slaves be what it will, they could not invent, with a common consent, the things that they one and all tell me with reference to the manner in which they have been treated by the man who has just left the estate, and his father, who for the last nineteen years have been sole sovereigns of their bodies and souls. The crops have satisfied the demands of the owners, who, living in Philadelphia, have been perfectly contented to receive a large income from their estate without apparently caring how it was earned.

Old Mr. Couper spoke with extreme kindness of his own people, and had evidently bestowed much humane and benevolent pains upon endeavors to better their condition. I asked him if he did not think the soil and climate of this part of Georgia admirably suited to the cultivation of the mulberry and the rearing of the silkworm; for it has appeared to me that hereafter silk may be made one of the most profitable products of this whole region: he said that that had long been his opinion, and he had at one time had it much at heart to try the experiment, and had proposed to Major Butler to join him in it, on a scale large enough to test it satisfactorily; but he said Mr. King opposed the scheme so persistently that of course it was impossible to carry it out, as his agency and cooperation were indispensable; and that in like manner he had suggested sowing turnip crops, and planting peachtrees for the benefit and use of the people on the Hampton estate, experiments which he had tried with excellent success on his own; but all these plans for the amelioration and progress of the people's physical condition had been obstructed and finally put entirely aside by old Mr. King and his son, who, as Mr. Couper said, appeared to give satisfaction to their employers, so it was not his business to find fault with them; he said, however, that the whole condition and treatment of the slaves had changed from the time of Major Butler's death, and that he thought it providential for the poor people that Mr.

King should have left the estate, and the young gentleman, the present owner, come down to look after the people.

He showed me his garden, from whence come the beautiful vegetables he had more than once supplied me with; in the midst of it was a very fine and flourishing date-palm-tree. After the garden we visited a charming, nicely kept poultry-yard, and I returned home much delighted with my visit and the kind good-humor of my host.

My letter has been lying unfinished for the last three days. I went on to visit the people at the Busson Hill settlement. I here found, among other noteworthy individuals, a female named Judy, whose two children belong to an individual called Joe, who has another wife, called Mary, at the rice-island. In one of the huts I went to leave some flannel, and rice, and sugar for a poor old creature called Nancy. She is exceedingly infirm and miserable, suffering from sore limbs and an ulcerated leg so cruelly that she can hardly find rest in any position from the constant pain she endures, and is quite unable to lie on her hard bed at night. As I bent over her to-day, trying to prop her into some posture where she might find some ease, she took hold of my hand, and with the tears streaming over her face, said, "I have worked every day through dew and damp, and sand and heat, and done good work; but oh, missis, me old and broken now; no tongue can tell how much I suffer." In the next cabin, which consisted of an inclosure called by courtesy a room, certainly not ten feet square, and inhabited by a woman called Dice, three grown-up human beings and eight children stow themselves by day and night.

After my return home a woman named Sophy came

to beg for some rice. In asking her about her husband and children, she said she had never had any husband; that she had had two children by a white man of the name of Walker, who was employed at the mill on the rice-island; she was in the hospital after the birth of the second child she bore this man, and at the same time two women, Judy and Sylla, of whose children Mr. King was the father, were recovering from their confinements. It was not a month since any of them had been delivered, when Mrs. King came to the hospital, had them all three severely flogged, a process which *she* personally super-intended, and then sent them to Five Pound—the swamp Botany Bay of the plantation, of which I have told you—with farther orders to the drivers to flog them every day for a week. Sophy went on to say that Isaac was her son by Driver Morris, who had forced her while she was in her miserable exile at Five Pound. Almost beyond my patience with this string of detestable details, I exclaimed —foolishly enough, heaven knows—"Ah! but don't you know—did nobody ever tell or teach any of you that it is a sin to live with men who are not your husbands?" Alas! what could the poor creature answer but what she did, seizing me at the same time vehemently by the wrist: "Oh yes, missis, we know—we know all about dat well enough; but we do any thing to get our poor flesh some rest from de whip; when he made me follow him into de bush, what use me tell him no? He have strength to make me." I have written down the woman's words; I wish I could write down the voice and look of abject misery with which they were spoken.

Another woman came in (Tema), carrying in her arms a child the image of the mulatto Bran; she came to beg for flannel. I asked her who was her husband. She said she was not married. Her child is the child of Bricklayer Temple, who has a wife at the rice-island. Flagrant acts of cruelty may be rare, but this ineffable state of utter degradation, this really *beastly* existence, is the normal condition of these men and women, and of that no one seems to take heed, nor have I ever heard it described, so as to form any adequate conception of it, till I found myself plunged into it.

It is Wednesday, the 20th of March; we can not stay here much longer; I wonder if I shall come back again! and whether, when I do, I shall find the trace of one idea of a better life left in these poor people's minds by my sojourn among them.

I must tell you that I have been delighted, surprised, and the very least perplexed, by the petition on the part of our young waiter, Aleck, that I will teach him to read. He is a very intelligent lad of about sixteen, and preferred his request with an urgent humility that was very touching. I told him I would think about it. I mean to do it; and yet, it is simply breaking the laws of the government under which I am living. The first offense of the sort is heavily fined, and the second more heavily fined, and for the third, one is sent to prison. I certainly intend to teach Aleck to read. I certainly won't tell Mr. Butler any thing about it.

I was stopped by one of our multitudinous Jennies with a request for some meat, and that I would help her with some clothes for Ben and Daphne, of whom she had the sole charge; these are two extremely pretty and interesting-looking mulatto children, whose resemblance to Mr. King had induced me to ask Mr. Butler, when first I saw them, if he did not think they must be his children. He said they were certainly like him, but Mr. King did not acknowledge the relationship. I asked Jenny who their mother was. "Minda." "Who their father?" "Mr. King." "What! old Mr. King?" "No, Mr. Roswell King." "Who told you so?" "Minda, who ought to know." "Mr. King denies it." "That's because he never has looked upon them, nor done a thing for them." "Well, but he acknowledged Renty as his son, why should he deny these?" "Because old master was here then when Renty was born, and he made Betty tell all about it, and Mr. King had to own it; but nobody knows any thing about this, and so he denies it"—with which information I rode home. You see from this that the people on the plantation themselves are much of my worthy neighbor Mr. Couper's mind, that the death of Major Butler was a great misfortune for the slaves on his estate.

I went to the hospital this afternoon to see if the condition of the poor people was at all improved since I had been last there; but nothing had been done. I suppose Mr. Gowen is waiting for Mr. Butler to come down in order to speak to him about it. I found some miserable new cases of women disabled by hard work. One poor thing, called Priscilla, had come out of the fields to-day scarcely able to crawl; she has been losing blood for a whole fortnight without intermission, and, until to-day, was laboring in the fields. Leah, another new face since I visited the hospital last, is lying quite helpless from exhaustion; she is advanced in her pregnancy, and doing task-work in the fields at the same time. What piteous existences, to be sure!

THE CARELESS DESOLATION

MARCH 1839

THE DAY BEFORE YESTERDAY, Mr. Butler and I rode together round most of the fields, and over the greater part of the plantation. It was a detestable process, the more so that he rode Montreal and I Miss Kate, and we had no small difficulty in managing them both. In the afternoon we had an equally detestable drive through the new wood paths to St. Annie's, and having accomplished all my errands among the people there, we crossed over certain sounds, and seas, and separating waters, to pay a neighborly visit to the wife of one of our adjacent planters.

How impossible it would be for you to conceive, even if I could describe, the careless desolation which pervaded the whole place; the shaggy unkempt grounds we passed through to approach the house; the ruinous, rackrent, tumble-down house itself; the untidy, slatternly, all but beggarly appearance of the mistress of the mansion herself. Mrs. Bryan favored me with the congratulations I have heard so many times on the subject of my having a white nursery-maid for my children. Of course, she went into the old subject of the utter incompetency of negro women to discharge such an office faithfully; but, in spite of her multiplied examples of their utter inefficiency, I believe the discussion ended by simply our both agreeing that ignorant negro girls of twelve years old are not as capable or trustworthy as well-trained white women of thirty.

Our row home was perfectly enchanting; for, though the morning's wind and (I suppose) the state of the tide had roughened the waters of the great river, and our passage was not as smooth as it might have been, the wind had died away, the evening air was deliciously still, and mild, and soft. A young slip of a moon glimmered just above the horizon, and "the stars climbed up the sapphire steps of heaven," while we made our way over the rolling, rushing, foaming waves, and saw to right and left the marsh fires burning in the swampy meadows, adding another colored light in the landscape to the amber-tinted lower sky and the violet arch above, and giving wild picturesqueness to the whole scene by throwing long flickering rays of flame upon the distant waters.

Sunday, the 24th. I read service again to-day to the people. You can not conceive any thing more impressive than the silent devotion of their whole demeanor while it lasted, nor more touching than the profound thanks with which they rewarded me when it was over, and they took their leave; and to-day they again left me with the utmost decorum of deportment, and without pressing a single petition or complaint such as they ordinarily thrust upon me on all other occasions, which seems to me an instinctive feeling of religious respect for the day and the business they have come upon, which does them infinite credit.

I am amused, but by no means pleased, at an entirely

new mode of pronouncing which Sally has adopted. Apparently the negro jargon has commended itself as euphonious to her infantile ears. She is now treating me to the most ludicrous and accurate imitations of it every time she opens her mouth. Of course I shall not allow this, comical as it is, to become a habit. It is a curious and sad enough thing to observe, as I have frequent opportunities of doing, the unbounded insolence and tyranny (of manner, of course it can go no farther) of the slaves toward each other. "Hi! you boy!" and "Hi! you girl!" shouted in an imperious scream, is the civilest mode of apostrophizing those at a distance from them; more frequently it is "You niggar, you hear? hi! you niggar!" And I assure you no contemptuous white intonation ever equaled the *prepotenza* of the despotic insolence of this address of these poor wretches to each other.

I have left my letter lying for a couple of days. I have been busy and tired; my walking and riding is becoming rather more laborious to me, for, though nobody here appears to do so, I am beginning to feel the relaxing influence of the spring.

Last Wednesday we drove to Hamilton, by far the finest estate on St. Simon's Island. The gentleman to whom it belongs lives, I believe, habitually in Paris. The negro huts on several of the plantations that we passed through were the most miserable human habitations I ever beheld, dirty, desolate, dilapidated dog-kennels out of which the negroes poured like black ants at our approach, and stood to gaze at us as we drove by. The planters' residences we passed were only three. It makes one ponder seriously when one thinks of the mere handful of white people on this island. In the midst of this large population of slaves, how absolutely helpless they would be if the blacks were to become restive! They could be destroyed to a man before human help could reach them from the main, or the tidings even of what was going on be carried across the surrounding waters.

We drove home by moonlight; and as we came toward the woods in the middle of the island, the fireflies glittered out from the dusky thickets as if some magical golden veil was every now and then shaken out into the darkness. The air was enchantingly mild and soft, and the whole way through the silvery night delightful.

In the afternoon I walked round the Point, and visited the houses of the people who are our nearest neighbors. I found poor Edie in sad tribulation at the prospect of resuming her field labor. It is really shameful treatment of a woman just after child-labor. She was confined exactly three weeks ago to-day, and she tells me she is ordered out to field-work on Monday. She seems to dread the approaching hardships of her task-labor extremely. Her baby was born dead, she thinks in consequence of a fall she had while carrying a heavy weight of water. She is suffering great pain in one of her legs and sides, and seems to me in a condition utterly unfit for any work, much less hoeing in the fields; but I dare not interfere to prevent this cruelty. She says she has already had to go out to work three weeks after her confinement with each of her other children, and does not complain of it as any thing special in her case. She says that is now the invariable rule of the whole plantation, though it used not to be so formerly.

To-day my visit to the Infirmary was marked by an event which has not occurred before—the death of one of the poor slaves while I was there. I found, on entering the first ward—to use a most inapplicable term for the dark, filthy, forlorn room I have so christened—an old negro called Friday lying on the ground. I asked what ailed him, and was told he was dying. I approached him, and perceived, from the glazed eyes and the feeble rattling breath, that he was at the point of expiring. His tattered shirt and trowsers barely covered his poor body; his appearance was that of utter exhaustion from age and feebleness; he had nothing under him but a mere handful of straw that did not cover the earth he was stretched on; and under his head, by way of pillow for his dying agony, two or three rough sticks just raising his skull a few inches from the ground. The flies were all gathering around his mouth, and not a creature was near him. There he lay—the worn-out slave, whose life had been spent in unrequited labor for me and mine, without one physical alleviation, one Christian solace, one human sympathy, to cheer him in his extremity—panting out the last breath of his wretched existence like some forsaken, overworked, wearied-out beast of burden, rotting where it falls! I bent over the poor awful human creature in the supreme hour of his mortality; and while my eyes, blinded with tears of unavailing pity and horror, were fixed upon him, there was a sudden quivering of the eyelids and falling of the jaw—and he was free.

In the next room I found a miserable, decrepid old negress, called Charity, lying sick, and I should think near too to die; but she did not think her work was over, much as she looked unfit for farther work on earth; but with feeble voice and beseeching hands implored me to have her work lightened when she was sent back to it from the hospital. She is one of the oldest slaves on the plantation, and has to walk to her field labor, and back again at night, a distance of nearly four miles. There

were an unusual number of sick women in the room to-
day; among them quite a young girl, daughter of Boat-
man Quash's, with a sick baby, who has a father, though
she has no husband. Poor thing! She looks like a mere
child herself. I returned home so very sad and heart-sick
that I could not rouse myself to the effort of going up to
St. Annie's with the presents I had promised the people
there. I sent Margery up in the wood-wagon with them,
and remained in the house with my thoughts, which
were none of the merriest.

CHURCH AT HOME

MARCH–APRIL 1839

IN THE EVENING poor Edie came up to the house to
see me, with an old negress called Sackey, who has been
one of the chief nurses on the island for many years. I
suppose she has made some application to Mr. Gowen
for a respite for Edie, on finding how terribly unfit she
is for work; or perhaps Mr. Butler, to whom I represented her case, may have ordered her reprieve; but she
came with much gratitude to me (who have, as far as I
know, had nothing to do with it), to tell me that she is
not to be sent into the field for another week. Old Sackey
fully confirmed Edie's account of the terrible hardships
the woman underwent in being thus driven to labor before they had recovered from childbearing. She said that
old Major Butler allowed the women at the rice-island
five weeks, and those here four weeks, to recover from
a confinement, and then never permitted them for some
time after they resumed their work to labor in the fields
before sunrise or after sunset; but Mr. King had altered
that arrangement, allowing the women at the rice-island
only four weeks, and those here only three weeks, for
their recovery; "and then, missis," continued the old

woman, "out into the field again, through dew and dry, as if nothing had happened; that is why, missis, so many of the women have falling of the womb and weakness in the back; and if he had continued on the estate, he would have utterly destroyed all the breeding women." Sometimes, after sending them back into the field at the expiration of their three weeks, they would work for a day or two, she said, and then fall down in the field with exhaustion, and be brought to the hospital almost at the point of death.

Yesterday, Sunday, I had my last service at home with these poor people; nearly thirty of them came, all clean, neat, and decent, in their dress and appearance. Sally had begged very hard to join the congregation, and upon the most solemn promise of remaining still she was admitted. The child's exquisite complexion, large gray eyes, and solemn and at the same time eager countenance, was such a contrast to their sable faces, so many of them so uncouth and yet all of them so pathetic, and some so sublime in their expression of patient suffering and religious fervor: their eyes never wandered from me and my child, who sat close by my knee, their little mistress, their future providence, my poor baby! At the end of the prayers, the tears were streaming over their faces, and one chorus of blessings rose round me and the child—farewell blessings, and prayers that we would return; and thanks so fervent in their incoherency, it was more than I could bear.

ALECK'S READING LESSON

APRIL 1839

AFTER ALL, we shall not leave Georgia so soon as I expected; we can not get off for at least another week. I am getting sick in spirit of my stay here; but I think the spring heat is beginning to affect me miserably, and I long for a cooler atmosphere. Here, on St. Simon's, the climate is perfectly healthy, and our neighbors, many of them, never stir from their plantations within reach of the purifying sea influence. But a land that grows magnolias is not fit for me—I was going to say magnolias and rattlesnakes.

I must give you an account of Aleck's first reading lesson, which took place at the same time that I gave Sally hers this morning. It was the first time he had had leisure to come, and it went off most successfully. He seems to me by no means stupid. I am very sorry he did not ask me to do this before; however, if he can master his alphabet before I go, he may, if chance favor him with the occasional sight of a book, help himself on by degrees.

I rode with Jack afterward, showing him where I wish paths to be cut and brushwood removed. I passed the new house, and again circumvented it meditatingly to discover its available points of possible future comeliness, but remained as convinced as ever that there are absolutely none. Within the last two days a perfect border of the dark blue *virginicum* has burst into blossom on each side of the road, fringing it with purple as far as one can look along it; it is lovely. I must tell you of something which has delighted me greatly. I told Jack yesterday that, if any of the boys liked, when they had done their tasks, to come and clear the paths that I want widened and trimmed, I would pay them a certain small sum per hour for their labor; and behold, three boys have come, having done their tasks early in the afternoon, to apply for *work* and *wages*: so much for a suggestion not barely twenty-four hours old, and so much for a prospect of compensation! My little workmen have brought me in from the woods three darling little rabbits which they have contrived to catch.

In the evening I attempted to walk out when the air was cool, but had to run precipitately back into the house to escape from the clouds of sand-flies that had settled on my neck and arms. The weather has suddenly become intensely hot; at least that is what it appears to me. After I had come in I had a visit from Venus and her daughter, a young girl of ten years old, for whom she begged a larger allowance of food, as, she said, what she received for her was totally inadequate to the girl's proper nourishment. I was amazed, upon inquiry, to find that three quarts of grits a week—that is not a pint a day—was considered a sufficient supply for children of her age. The mother said her child was half-famished on it, and it seemed to me terribly little.

The other day, Psyche (the pretty under nurse, the

poor thing whose story I wrote from the rice plantation) asked me if her mother and brothers might be allowed to come and see her when we are gone away. I asked her some questions about them, and she told me that one of her brothers, who belonged to Mr. King, was hired by that gentleman to a Mr. G——, of Darien, and that, upon the latter desiring to purchase him, Mr. King had sold the man without apprising him or any one member of his family that he had done so—a humane proceeding that makes one's blood boil when one hears of it. He had owned the man ever since he was a boy. Psyche urged me very much to obtain an order permitting her to see her mother and brothers. I will try and obtain it for her; but there seems generally a great objection to the visits of slaves from neighboring plantations. The more I see of this frightful and perilous social system, the more I feel that those who live in the midst of it must make their whole existence one constant precaution against danger of some sort or other.

I have given Aleck a second reading lesson with Sally, who takes an extreme interest in his newly acquired alphabetical lore. He is a very quick and attentive scholar, and I should think a very short time would suffice to teach him to read; but, alas! I have not even that short time. When I had done with my class I rode off with Jack, who has become quite an expert horseman, and rejoices in being lifted out of the immediate region of snakes by the length of his horse's legs. I cantered through the new wood paths, and took a good sloping galop through the pine land to St. Annie's. I came home quite tired with the heat, though my ride was not a long one.

Just as I had taken off my habit and was preparing to

start off with Margery and the chicks for Jones's in the wood-wagon, old Dorcas, one of the most decrepid, rheumatic, and miserable old negresses from the farther end of the plantation, called in to beg for some sugar. She had walked the whole way from her own settlement, and seemed absolutely exhausted then, and yet she had to walk all the way back. It was not otherwise than slightly meritorious in me to take her up in the wagon and endure her abominable dirt and foulness in the closest proximity, rather than let her drag her poor old limbs all that way back; but I was glad when we gained her abode and lost her company.

The people at Jones's had done their work at half past three. Most of the houses were tidy and clean, so were many of the babies. On visiting the cabin of an exceed-ingly decent woman called Peggy, I found her, to my surprise, possessed of a fine large Bible. She told me her husband, Carpenter John, can read, and that she means to make him teach her. The fame of Aleck's literature has evidently reached Jones's, and they are not afraid to tell me that they can read or wish to learn to do so. This poor woman's health is miserable; I never saw a more weakly, sickly looking creature. She says she has been broken down ever since the birth of her last child. I asked her how soon after her confinement she went out into the field to work again. She answered very quickly, but with a deep sigh, "Three weeks, missis; de usual time." As I was going away, a man named Martin came up, and with great vehemence besought me to give him a Prayer-book. In the evening he came down to fetch it, and to show me that he can read. I was very much pleased to see that they had taken my hint about nailing wooden slats across the windows of their poor huts, to prevent the constant ingress of the poultry. This in itself will produce an immense difference in the cleanliness and comfort of their wretched abodes. In one of the huts I found a broken looking-glass; it was the only piece of furniture of the sort that I had yet seen among them. The woman who owned it was, I am sorry to say, peculiarly untidy and dirty, and so were her children.

I drove home, late in the afternoon, through the sweet-smelling woods, that are beginning to hum with the voice of thousands of insects. My troop of volunteer workmen is increased to five—five lads working for my wages after they have done their task-work; and this evening, to my no small amazement, Driver Bran came down to join them for an hour, after working all day at Five Pound, which certainly shows zeal and energy.

I had another snake encounter in my ride this morning. Just as I had walked my horse through the swamp, and while contemplating ruefully its naked aspect, a huge black snake wriggled rapidly across the path, and I pulled my reins tight and opened my mouth wide with horror.

I rode home very fast, in spite of the exquisite fragrance of the wild cherry blossoms, the carpets and curtains of wild flowers, among which a sort of glorified dandelion glowed conspicuously—dandelions such as I should think grew in the garden of Eden, if there were any at all there. I passed the finest magnolia that I have yet seen; it was magnificent, and I suppose had been spared for its beauty, for it grew in the very middle of a cotton-field.

I have spent the whole afternoon at home; my "gang" is busily at work again. Sawney, one of them, came to join it nearly at sundown, not having got through his day's task before. In watching and listening to these lads, I was constantly struck with the insolent tyranny of their demeanor toward each other. This is almost a universal characteristic of the manner of the negroes among themselves. They are diabolically cruel to animals too, and they seem to me, as a rule, hardly to know the difference between truth and falsehood. These detestable qualities, which I constantly hear attributed to them as innate and inherent in their race, appear to me the direct result of their condition. The individual exceptions among them are, I think, quite as many as would be found, under similar circumstances, among the same number of white people.

In considering the whole condition of the people on this plantation, it appears to me that the principal hardships fall to the lot of the women—that is, the principal physical hardships. The very young members of the community are of course idle and neglected; the very, very old, idle and neglected too; the middle-aged men do not appear to me overworked, and lead a mere animal existence, in itself not peculiarly cruel or distressing, but involving a constant element of fear and uncertainty, and the trifling evils of unrequited labor, ignorance the most profound (to which they are condemned by law), and the unutterable injustice which precludes them from all the merits and all the benefits of voluntary exertion, and the progress that results from it. If they are absolutely unconscious of these evils, then they are not very ill-off brutes, always barring the chance of being given or sold away from their mates or their young—processes which even brutes do not always relish. I am very much struck with the vein of melancholy, which assumes almost a poetical tone in some of the things they say. Did I tell you of that poor old decrepid creature Dorcas, who came to beg some sugar of me the other day? saying, as she took up my watch from the table and looked at it, "Ah! I need not look at this; I have almost done with time!"

MR. COUPER & THE CHURCH

APRIL 1839

LAST NIGHT I RECEIVED a present from Mrs. Fraser of a drum-fish, which animal I had never beheld before, and which seemed to me first cousin to the great Leviathan. It is to be eaten, and is certainly the biggest fish food I ever saw; however, every thing is in proportion, and the prawns that came with it are upon a similarly extensive scale; this magnificent piscatorial bounty was accompanied by a profusion of Hamilton green peas, really a munificent supply.

I went out early after breakfast with Jack hunting for new paths; we rode all along the road by Jones's Creek, and most beautiful it was. We skirted the plantation burial-ground, and a dismal place it looked; the cattle trampling over it in every direction, except where Mr. King had had an inclosure put up round the graves of two white men who had worked on the estate. They were strangers, and of course utterly indifferent to the people here; but by virtue of their white skins, their resting-place was protected from the hoofs of the cattle, while the parents and children, wives, husbands, brothers and sisters, of the poor slaves, sleeping beside them, might see the graves of those they loved trampled upon and browsed over, desecrated and defiled, from morning till night. There is something intolerably cruel in this disdainful denial of a common humanity pursuing these wretches even when they are hid beneath the earth.

I spent the afternoon at home. I dread going out twice a day now, on account of the heat and the sand-flies. While I was sitting by the window, Abraham, our cook, went by with some most revolting-looking "raw material" (part, I think, of the interior of the most monstrous drum-fish of which I have told you). I asked him, with considerable disgust, what he was going to do with it; he replied, "Oh! We colored people eat it, missis." Said I, "Why do you say we colored people?" "Because, missis, white people won't touch what we too glad of." "That," said I, "is because you are poor, and do not often have meat to eat, not because you are colored, Abraham; rich white folks will not touch what poor white folks are too glad of; it has nothing in the world to do with color; and if there were white people here worse off than you (amazing and inconceivable suggestion, I fear), they would be glad to eat what you perhaps would not touch." Profound pause of meditation on the part of Abraham, wound up by a considerate "Well, missis, I suppose so;" after which he departed with the horrid-looking offal.

To-day—Saturday—My rides are drawing to a close, and even were I to remain here this must be the case, unless I got up and rode under the stars in the cool of the night. This afternoon I was obliged to drive up to St. Annie's: I had promised the people several times that I would do so. I went after dinner and as late as I could, and found very considerable improvement in the whole condition of the place; the houses had all been swept, and some of them actually scoured. The children were all quite tolerably clean; they had put slats across all their windows, and little chicken-gates to the doors to keep out the poultry. There was a poor woman lying in one of the cabins in a wretched condition. She begged for a bandage, but I do not see of what great use that can be to her, as long as she has to hoe in the fields so many hours a day, which I can not prevent.

Returning home, Israel undertook to pilot me across the cotton-fields into the pine land. He said the rattle-snakes were very numerous, and were found in every direction all over the plantation, but that they did not become really vicious until quite late in the summer; until then, it appears that they generally endeavor to make off if one meets them, but during the intense heats of the latter part of July and August they never think of escaping, but at any sight or sound which they may consider inimical they instantly coil themselves for a spring. The most intolerable proceeding on their part, however, that he described, was their getting up into the trees, and either coiling themselves in or depending from the branches. There is something too revolting in the idea of serpents looking down upon one from the shade of the trees to which one may betake one's self for shelter in the dreadful heat of the Southern midsummer. The moccasin snake, which is nearly as deadly as the rattle-snake, abounds all over the island.

In the evening I had a visit from Mr. Couper and Mr. Bartow, who officiates to-morrow at our small island church. The conversation I had with these gentlemen was sad enough. They seem good, and kind, and amiable men, and I have no doubt are conscientious in their ca-

147

pacity of slaveholders; but to one who has lived outside this dreadful atmosphere, the whole tone of their discourse has a morally muffled sound, which one must hear to be able to conceive. Mr. Bartow told me that the people on this plantation not going to church was the result of a positive order from Mr. King, who had peremptorily forbidden their doing so, and of course to have infringed that order would have been to incur severe corporal chastisement. Bishop Bowen, it seems, had advised that there should be periodical preaching on the plantations, which, said Mr. Bartow, would have obviated any necessity for the people of different estates congregating at any given point at stated times, which might perhaps be objectionable, and at the same time would meet the reproach which was now beginning to be directed toward Southern planters as a class, of neglecting the eternal interest of their dependents. But Mr. King had equally objected to this. Poor people, one and all, but especially poor oppressors of the oppressed!

To-day is Sunday, and I have been to the little church on the island. It is the second time since I came down to the South that I have been to a place of worship. A curious little incident prefaced my going thither this morning. I had desired Israel to get my horse ready and himself to accompany me, as I meant to ride to church; and you can not imagine any thing droller than his horror and dismay when he at length comprehended that my purpose was to attend divine service in my riding-habit. I asked him what was the trouble; for, though I saw something was creating a dreadful convulsion in his mind, I had no idea what it was till he told me, adding that he had never seen such a thing on St. Simon's in his life.

148

I was standing at the open window speaking to him about the horses, and telling him to get ready to ride with me, when George, another of the men, went by with a shade or visor to his cap exactly the shape of the one I left behind at the North, and for want of which I have been suffering severely from the intense heat and glare of the sun for the last week. I asked him to hand me his cap, saying, "I want to take the pattern of that shade." Israel exclaimed, "Oh, missis, not to-day; let him leave the cap with you to-morrow, but don't cut pattern on de Sabbath day!" It seemed to me a much more serious matter to offend this scruple than the prejudice with regard to praying in a riding-habit; still, it had to be done. "Do you think it wrong, Israel," said I, "to work on Sunday?" "Yes, missis, parson tell we so." "Then, Israel, be sure you never do it. Did your parson never tell you that your conscience was for yourself and not for your neighbors, Israel?" "Oh yes, missis, he tell we that too." "Then mind that too, Israel." The shade was cut out and stitched upon my cap, and protected my eyes from the fierce glare of the sun and sand as I rode to church. On our way we came to a field where the young corn was coming up. The children were in the field—little living scarecrows—watching it, of course, as on a weekday, to keep off the birds. I made Israel observe this, who replied, "Oh, missis, if de people's corn left one whole day not watched, not one blade of it remain to-morrow; it must be watched, missis." "What, on the Sabbath-day, Israel?" "Yes, missis, or else we lose it all."

You can not imagine any thing wilder or more beautiful than the situation of the little rustic temple in the woods where I went to worship to-day, with the magnificent live oaks standing round it and its picturesque

149

burial-ground. The disgracefully neglected state of the latter, its broken and ruinous inclosure, and its shaggy, weed-grown graves, tell a strange story of the residents of this island, who are content to leave the resting-place of their dead in so shocking a condition. In the tiny little chamber of a church, the grand old Litany of the Episcopal Church of England was not a little shorn of its ceremonial stateliness; clerk there was none, nor choir, nor organ, and the clergyman did duty for all, giving out the hymn and then singing it himself, followed as best might be by the uncertain voices of his very small congregation, the smallest I think I ever saw gathered in a Christian place of worship, even counting a few of the negroes who had ventured to place themselves standing at the back of the church—an infringement on their part upon the privileges of their betters, as Mr. Bartow generally preaches a second sermon to them after the *white* service, to which, as a rule, they are not admitted.

On leaving the church, I mounted my horse, and resumed my ride and my conversation with Israel. He told me that Mr. King's great objection to the people going to church was their meeting with the slaves from the other plantations; and one reason, he added, that he did not wish them to do that was, that they trafficked and bartered away the cooper's wares, tubs, piggins, etc., made on the estate. I think, however, from every thing I hear of that gentleman, that the mere fact of the Hampton people coming in contact with the slaves of other plantations would be a thing he would have deprecated. As a severe disciplinarian, he was probably right.

In the course of our talk, a reference I made to the Bible, and Israel's answer that he could not read, made me ask him why his father had never taught any of his sons to read; old Jacob, I know, can read. What followed I shall never forget. He began by giving all sorts of childish unmeaning excuses and reasons for never having tried to learn—became confused and quite incoherent—and then, suddenly stopping, and pulling up his horse, said, with a look and manner that went to my very heart, "Missis, what for me learn to read? Me have no prospect!" I explained to him that, though indeed "without prospect" in some respects, yet reading might avail him much to better his condition, moral, mental, and physical. He listened very attentively, and was silent for a minute; after which he said, "All you say very true, missis, and me sorry now me let de time pass; but you know what de white man dat goberns de estate him seem to like and favor, dat de people find out bery soon and do it; now Massa King, him neber favor our reading, him not like it; likely as not he lick you if he find you reading; or, if you wish to teach your children, him always say, 'Pooh! teach 'em to *read*? Teach 'em to *work*!' According to dat, we neber paid much attention to it; but now it will be different; it was different in former times. De old folks of my father and mother's time could read more than we can, and I expect de people will dare to give some thought to it again now." This man Israel is a remarkably fine fellow in every way, with a frank, open, and most intelligent countenance, which rises before me with its look of quiet sadness whenever I think of these words (and they haunt me), "I have no prospect."

On my arrival at home I found that a number of the people, not knowing I had gone to church, had come up to the house, hoping that I would read prayers to them, and had not gone back to their homes, but waited to see me. I could not bear to disappoint them, for many of them had come from the farthest settlements on the estate; and so I took off my habit, and had them all in, and read the afternoon service to them. When it was over, two of the women—Venus and Tressa—asked if they might be permitted to go to the nursery and see the children. Their account of the former condition of the estate was a corroboration of Israel's. They said that the older slaves on the plantation had been far better off than the younger ones of the present day; that Major Butler was considerate and humane to his people; and that the women were especially carefully treated. But they said Mr. King had ruined all the young women with working them too soon after their confinements; and as for the elder ones, he would kick them, curse them, turn their clothes over their heads, flog them unmercifully himself, and abuse them shamefully, no matter what condition they were in. They both ended with fervent thanks to God that he had left the estate, and rejoicing that we had come, and, above all, that we "had made young missis for them." Venus went down on her knees, exclaiming, "Oh, missis, I glad now; and when I am dead, I glad in my grave that you come to us and bring us little missis."

THE LAST RIDE

APRIL 1839

I RODE TO-DAY through all my wood paths for the last time with Jack, and I think I should have felt quite melancholy at taking leave of them and him but for the apparition of a large black snake, which filled me with disgust and nipped my other sentiments in the bud. Not a day passes now that I do not encounter one or more of these hateful reptiles; it is curious how much more odious they are to me than the alligators that haunt the mud banks of the river round the rice plantation. It is true that there is something very dreadful in the thick shapeless mass, uniform in color almost to the black slime on which it lies basking, and which you hardly detect till it begins to move. But even those ungainly crocodiles never sickened me as those rapid, lithe, and sinuous serpents do. Did I ever tell you that the people at the rice plantation caught a young alligator and brought it to the house, and it was kept for some time in a tub of water? It was an ill-tempered little monster; it used to set up its back like a cat when it was angry; and open its long jaws in a most vicious manner.

In the afternoon we paid a long visit to Mr. Couper.

It is extremely interesting to me to talk with him about the negroes; he has spent so much of his life among them, has managed them so humanely, and apparently so successfully, that his experience is worthy of all attention. And yet it seems to me that it is impossible, or rather, perhaps, for those very reasons it is impossible, for him ever to contemplate them in any condition but that of slavery. He thinks them very like the Irish, and instanced their subserviency, their flattering, their lying, and pilfering, as traits common to the characters of both peoples. But I can not persuade myself that in both cases, and certainly in that of the negroes, these qualities are not in great measure the result of their condition. He says that he considers the extremely low diet of the negroes one reason for the absence of crimes of a savage nature among them; most of them do not touch meat the year round.

His statement that it is impossible to bribe the negroes to work on their own account with any steadiness may be generally true, but admits of quite exceptions enough to throw doubt upon its being natural supineness in the race rather than the inevitable consequence of denying them the entire right to labor for their own profit. Their laziness seems to me the necessary result of their primary wants being supplied, and all progress denied them. Mr. Couper said that he had offered a bribe of twenty dollars apiece, and the use of a pair of oxen, for the clearing of a certain piece of land, to the men on his estate, and found the offer quite ineffectual to procure the desired result; the land was subsequently cleared as usual task-work under the lash. Now, certainly, we have among Mr. Butler's people instances of men who have made very considerable sums of money by boat-building in their leisure hours, and the instances of almost life-long, persevering, stringent labor, by which slaves have at length purchased their own freedom and that of their wives and children, are on record in numbers sufficient to prove that they are capable of severe sustained effort of the most patient and heroic kind for that great object, liberty.

One thing that Mr. Couper said seemed to me to prove rather too much. He declared that his son, objecting to the folks on his plantation going about bareheaded, had at one time offered a reward of a dollar to those who should habitually wear hats without being able to induce them to do so, which he attributed to sheer careless indolence; but I think it was merely the force of habit of going uncovered rather than absolute laziness. The universal testimony of all present at this conversation was in favor of the sweetness of temper and natural gentleness of disposition of the negroes; but these characteristics they seemed to think less inherent than the result of diet and the other lowering influences of their condition; and it must not be forgotten that on the estate of this wise and kind master a formidable conspiracy was organized among his slaves.

We rowed home through a world of stars, the steadfast ones set in the still blue sky, and the flashing swathes of phosphoric light turned up by our oars and keel in the smooth blue water. It was lovely.

PRAYERS & ADMONITIONS

APRIL 1839

I DROVE TO CHURCH to-day in the wood-wagon, with Jack and Aleck, Hector being our charioteer, in a gilt guard-chain and pair of slippers to match as the Sabbatic part of his attire. The love of dirty finery seems to exist in men and women alike; but I think all savage men rejoice, even more than their women, in personal ornamentation. The negroes certainly show the same strong predilection for finery with their womenkind. The air of the church was perfectly thick with sand-flies; and the disgraceful carelessness of the congregation in responding and singing the hymns, and the entire neglect of the Prayer-book regulations for kneeling, disturbed and displeased me even more than the last time I was at church.

I had service at home in the afternoon, and my congregation was much more crowded than usual; for I believe there is no doubt at last that we shall leave Georgia this week. Having given way so much before when I thought I was praying with these poor people for the last time, I suppose I had, so to speak, expended my emotion, and I was much more composed and quiet than when I took leave of them before. After prayers I gave my poor people a parting admonition, and many charges to remember me and all I had tried to teach them during my stay. They promised with one voice to mind and do all that "missis tell we;" and with many a parting benediction, and entreaties to me to return, they went their way.

In the afternoon I walked out, and passed many of the people, who are now beginning, whenever they see me, to say "Good-by, missis!" Many of them were clean and tidy, and decent in their appearance to a degree that certainly bore strong witness to the temporary efficacy of my influence in this respect. I met Abraham, and thought that, in a quiet *tête-à-tête*, and with the pathetic consideration of my near departure to assist me, I could get him to confess the truth about the disappearance of the mutton; but he persisted in the legend of its departure through the locked door.

I returned home, finding the heat quite oppressive. Late in the evening, when the sun had gone down a long time, I thought I would try and breathe the fresh sea air, but the atmosphere was thick with sand-flies, which drove me in at last from standing listening to the roar of the Atlantic on Little St. Simon's Island, the wooded belt that fends off the ocean surges from the north side of Great St. Simon's. It is a wild little sand-heap, covered with thick forest growth, and belongs to Mr. Butler.

FAREWELLS & PONDERING FATE

APRIL 1839

WE SHALL LEAVE this place next Thursday or Friday, and there will be an end to this record; meantime I am fulfilling all sorts of last duties, and especially those of taking leave of my neighbors, by whom the neglect of a farewell visit would be taken much amiss. On Sunday I rode to a place called Frederica to call on a Mrs. Abbott, who came to see me some time ago. I rode straight through the island by the main road that leads to the little church.

How can I describe to you the exquisite spring beauty that is now adorning these woods, the variety of the fresh, new-born foliage, the fragrance of the sweet, wild perfumes that fill the air? Honeysuckles twine round every tree; the ground is covered with a low, white-blossomed shrub more fragrant than lilies of the valley. The accacuas are swinging their silver censers under the green roof of these wood temples; every stump is like a classical altar to the sylvan gods, garlanded with flowers; every post, or stick, or slight stem, like a Bacchante's thyrsus, twined with wreaths of ivy and wild vine, waving in the tepid wind. Beautiful butterflies flicker like flying flowers among the bushes, and gorgeous birds, like winged jewels, dart from the boughs, and—and—a huge ground snake slid like a dark ribbon across the path while I was stopping to enjoy all this deliciousness, and so I became less enthusiastic, and cantered on past the little deserted church-yard, with the new-made grave beneath its grove of noble oaks, and a little farther on reached Mrs. Abbott's cottage, half hidden in the midst of ruins and roses.

I sat for a long time with Mrs. Abbott, and a friend of hers staying with her, lately from Florida. We had a long discussion on the subject of slavery, and they took, as usual, the old ground of justifying the system, where it was administered with kindness and indulgence. They were very patient of my strong expressions of reprobation of the whole system, and Mrs. Abbott, bidding me good-by, said that, for aught she could tell, I might be right, and might have been led down here by Providence to be the means of some great change in the condition of the poor colored people.

I rode home pondering on the strange fate that has brought me to this place so far from where I was born, this existence so different in all its elements from that of my early years and former associations. On my return home I found a most enchanting bundle of flowers, sent to me by Mrs. Grant; pomegranate blossoms, roses, honeysuckle.

Wednesday, 17th April. I rode to-day, after breakfast, to Mrs. Demere's, another of my neighbors, who lives full twelve miles off. During the last two miles of my expedition I had the white sand hillocks and blue line of the Atlantic in view. The house at which I called was a tumble-down barrack of a dwelling in the woods, with a sort of poverty-stricken pretentious air about it, like sundry "proud planters'" dwellings that I have seen. I was received by the sons as well as the lady of the house, and could not but admire the lordly rather than manly indifference with which these young gentlemen, in gay guard chains and fine attire, played the gallants, while filthy, barefooted, half-naked negro women brought in refreshments, and stood all the while fanning the cake, and sweetmeats, and their young masters, as if they had been all the same sort of stuff. I felt ashamed for the lads. I took my leave and rode home. I met my babies in the wood-wagon, and took Sally up before me, and gave her a good gallop home. Having reached the house with the appetite of a twenty-four miles' ride, I found no preparation for dinner, and not so much as a boiled potato to eat, and the sole reply to my famished and disconsolate exclamations was, "Being that you order none, missis, I not know." I had forgotten to order my dinner, and my *slaves*, unauthorized, had not ventured to prepare any, and so I fasted till some tea could be got for me.

This was the last letter I wrote from the plantation, and I never returned there.